America's Top Internet Job Sites

By Ron and Caryl Krannich

America's Top
Internet Job Sites

Second Edition

Ron and Caryl Krannich, Ph.Ds

IMPACT PUBLICATIONS
Manassas Park, Virginia

America's Top Internet Job Sites

Second Edition

Library of Congress Cataloguing-in-Publication Data

Krannich, Ronald L.
    America's top internet job sites: the click and easy guide to
  finding a job online / Ronald L. Krannich, Caryl Rae Krannich –
  2nd Edition
        p. cm.
    Includes bibliographical references and index.
    ISBN 1-57023-210-5
    1. Job hunting – Computer network resources. 2. Internet.
  I. Krannich, Caryl Rae. II. Title

HF5382.7 .K69 2003
025.06'331702 – dc21   200311055

Publisher: For information on Impact Publications, including current and forthcoming publications, authors, press kits, online bookstore, and submission requirements, visit www.impactpublications.com.

Publicity/Rights: For information on publicity, author interviews, and subsidiary rights, contact the Media Relations Department: Tel. 703-361-7300, Fax 703-335-9486, or email info@impactpublications.com.

Sales/Distribution: All bookstore sales are handled through Impact's trade distributor: National Book Network, 15200 NBN Way, Blue Ridge Summit, PA 17214, Tel. 1-800-462-6420. All other sales and distribution inquiries should be directed to the publisher: Sales Department, IMPACT PUBLICATIONS, 9104-N Manassas Drive, Manassas Park, VA 20111-5211, Tel. 703-361-7300, Fax 703-335-9486, or email info@impactpublications.com.

Contents

Preface

FINDING A JOB TODAY IS BOTH easier and more difficult and frustrating than ever before. It looks and feels easier because of the wealth of employment information and free services readily available to job seekers on the Internet, 24 hours a day and with just a click of a mouse. At the same time, it can be more difficult and frustrating because you may become overwhelmed with the information, you may have difficulty choosing quality resources, your competition may be using the same online resources, and employers may demand more evidence of performance from a larger pool of qualified candidates. If you want to become a savvy job seeker, you need to wisely integrate the Internet into your job search and clearly communicate to employers that you have the requisite skills and abilities to do the job.

While the Internet should play an important role in your job search – from researching companies to applying for jobs online – it should never substitute for the job search itself. Indeed, too many job seekers become preoccupied with conducting an online job search rather than organizing an overall effective job search that includes both online and offline elements. Not surprisingly, many digital-oriented job seekers would rather sit behind a computer screen searching for job listings and applying online than picking up the telephone or meeting with individuals about their job search.

We wrote this book because we saw a need to approach both the Internet and the job search from a different, and more balanced, perspective. Too often, too much misplaced emphasis and hype are given to conducting a job search on the Internet. While we believe the Internet can play a critical role in any job search, we also believe it should be fully integrated into a well organized and purposeful job search process – from beginning to end. However, during the past few years, numerous employment websites, primarily funded by employers and recruiters, have promoted a questionable job search model that primarily benefits employers, recruiters, and website entrepreneurs rather than individual job seekers. Operated as free job boards for job seekers, these sites coach visitors to enter their resumes online and search for job listings. Essentially a "classified ad and resume submission" approach to the job search, many of these sites work especially well for employers who can now use the Internet to inexpensively and effectively cast a much wider net for locating, persuading, screening, and recruiting candidates. But this approach is not necessarily in the best interests of many job seekers who also should be engaged in several other job search activities **before** submitting their resume online, surveying job listings, and applying for jobs.

America's Top Internet Job Sites is primarily written for job seekers rather than for employers, recruiters, or Internet entrepreneurs who operate employment websites. From beginning to end, we organized the book around one key question – *How can job seekers best benefit from using the Internet or particular employment websites in their job search?* We're talking about **using the Internet in your job search** rather than **conducting an Internet job search** – an important distinction for organizing this book and assessing individual websites. Our single-minded pursuit of this **benefit question** for job seekers meant organizing the book around the **job search** rather than focusing on identifying, classifying, and judging the superficial visual elements or the "traffic" rates of employment websites.

From the perspective of employers, recruiters, and webmasters, these are **recruitment websites**. From the perspective of job seekers, these same sites are **job search websites**. The differing perspectives arise from the differences in expected benefits. Ironically, no one really knows, beyond a few anecdotal success stories, how effective these same sites are for job seekers. In fact, many job seekers remain frustrated in using these sites. They complain of receiving few if any invitations to job interviews based on their Internet activities. Yet, few job seekers really know how to conduct an effective job search either online or offline.

For us, as well as many experienced career professionals, **effectiveness for job seekers** is found in following a clearly defined job search process in which the Internet plays an important, but not an all-encompassing, role. It all begins with self-assessment and goal setting – not with resumes, letters, and applications. We believe you are best served by a book that integrates the Internet into each sequential step of the job search – assessment, goal setting, research, networking, resume and letter writing, interviewing, and negotiating compensation and terms of employment. Rather than focus primarily on the largest and most popular employment websites, we identify websites that can play important roles in each step of your job search. For in the end, the most critical steps in this whole process take place offline – job interviews and salary negotiations. After all, employers don't hire people off the Internet – they only screen them for interviews, which take place in face-to-face settings. The Internet can help you get to and prepare you for the job interview, but from there you are essentially offline and on your own.

One technical note before you start using this book. You may discover that some of our web addresses no longer work. That would not surprise us since so many websites come and go or change URLs as they become absorbed into other sites. Many of these businesses have a very short life-span or become "cob webs" with little or no expensive maintenance. If you can't connect to some of our sites, chances are they've gone out of business. We expect 20 to 30 percent of our sites will disappear within three years.

We wish you well with your online job search adventure. You'll find an absolutely incredible amount of employment information and services on the Internet which can become very seductive and time consuming. Whatever you do, approach the many websites with the wisdom of someone who understands how the online information and services can best be integrated into your job search. While anyone can find a job, your single-minded goal should be to find a job that you do well and enjoy doing – one that allows you to pursue your passion. The Internet should help you find the perfect "fit" between your interests, skills, and goals and the needs of employers. May you find your perfect job and career with the help of the many websites identified in the following chapters.

Ron and Caryl Krannich

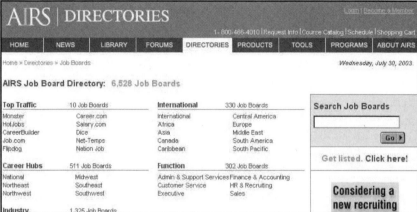

AIRS | DIRECTORIES

Login | Become a Member

1-800-466-4010 | Request Info | Course Catalog | Schedule | Shopping Cart

| HOME | NEWS | LIBRARY | FORUMS | DIRECTORIES | PRODUCTS | TOOLS | PROGRAMS | ABOUT AIRS |

Home » Directories » Job Boards

Wednesday, July 30, 2003

AIRS Job Board Directory: 6,528 Job Boards

Top Traffic	10 Job Boards
Monster	Career.com
HotJobs	Salary.com
CareerBuilder	Dice
Job.com	Net-Temps
Flipdog	Nation Job

International	330 Job Boards	
International		Central America
Africa		Europe
Asia		Middle East
Canada		South America
Caribbean		South Pacific

Career Hubs	511 Job Boards
National	Midwest
Northeast	Southeast
Northwest	Southwest

Function	302 Job Boards	
Admin & Support Services	Finance & Accounting
Customer Service	HR & Recruiting
Executive	Sales

Search Job Boards

Go! ▶

Get listed. **Click here!**

Considering a new recruiting

Industry   1,325 Job Boards

EMPLOYERS

**POST JOBS
SEARCH RESUMES
LOG IN**

ENTER HERE

monster®

never settle™

Search Jobs   **POST YOUR RESUME**   **MY MONSTER LOGIN**   **GET CAREER ADVICE**

Monster Works...for you.
Whatever you're looking for in a job, Monster can help you find it. With the best job search tools and career advice on the planet...we'll show you how to land the job that's right for you. Click here if you're new to Monster

Career Marketplace
Serious tools for
the serious career.
Put them to work
for you now. ▶

Featured Employers
Advertise Here ▶

Be Your Own
Employer ▶

Jennifer's Story:

From Local
Nurse to
National
Explorer

Give Us Your Opinion!
When was the last time you got a raise?
○ 0-5 months ago.

IMPACT PUBLICATIONS
The Career & Travel Resource Center

1-800-361-1055 or 703-361-7300

| Home | Impact Books | Career Store | Travel Store | Catalogs | eBook Store |

Search Career: Career Mgmt/HR   GO!   Search Travel: Accommodations   GO!

SEARCH&Shop

GO!

Login Register
Your Shopping Cart
<Basket Empty>

CAREERstore

TRAVELstore

Login   Register

Career & Business Store

Your gateway to today's most useful books, videos, software, and other products relevant to job seekers, employers, and students. Includes career exploration, job search activities (resumes, cover letters, interviewing, networking, and negotiating salary), career development, recruitment, education (college testing, admissions, and finance), and entrepreneurship.

9 Downloadable Catalogs

Travel Store

Discover fabulous travel destinations and adventures around the world with hundreds of books geared to both leisure and business travelers. From budget to super-luxury, selections focus on great shopping, dining,

1

The Intriguing World of Internet Job Sites

OST JOB SEEKERS AND EMPLOYERS need to incorporate the Internet in their job search and hiring activities. But how to do this effectively remains a major challenge. For example, how much time and effort should you devote to Internet-related job search activities? Which websites are likely to yield the most useful information, advice, and contacts that lead to job interviews and offers? How can you best relate traditional job search activities, such as face-to-face networking, to online job search activities such as posting resumes and joining discussion groups? How do top employers best use the Internet for recruiting? Which employment websites do they find most useful? Are you wisely using the Internet in your job search? These and many other "effectiveness" questions are central to this new edition of *America's Top Internet Job Sites*.

Job Sites Galore But Where to Go

By some estimates, more than 25,000 non-employer websites now focus on employment. Many of these sites manage over seven million online resumes for connecting job seekers with employers. These range from dozens of mega employment sites designed for both employers and job seekers, such as Monster, DirectEmployers, CareerBuilder, and HotJobs, to highly specialized websites that test, coach, or assist job seekers in blasting their resumes to thousands of employers, such as CareerLab, CertifiedCareerCoaches, and BlastMyResume. If you also include employment information found on the websites of employers, the number of job-related websites may well increase to over 500,000! Indeed, the trend today is for more and more employers to develop an employment section on their company website in order to recruit candidates directly rather than use commercial employment websites.

Welcome to the wonderful, excessively hyped, and seemingly chaotic world of employment information, an electronic world of great promises and numerous pitfalls. Easily accessible, the quality and usefulness of this world is by no means certain, but it's a world worth exploring and incorporating in your job search. Exploited intelligently, this world can greatly enhance each step of your job search.

Facing a Daunting Task

So, you're well advised to incorporate the Internet in your job search, but where should you go once you're on the Internet? How can you best use this resource without wasting a great deal of time on random activities that may generate false hopes with few useful outcomes? What expectations should you have when using the Internet for finding a job? For job seekers, the ultimate goal or outcome should be to connect with the right employer who invites you to a job interview and offers you a job. Unfortunately, many job seekers get lost along the way as they wander aimlessly in a chaotic click and sound-bite arena. Lacking clear goals when using the Internet, they easily become distracted as they lose focus on what's really important to a job search. Jumping from one "interesting" website to another, they forget there is indeed a forest among all the trees they've been having fun swinging from. The forest is the job search, which involves a very well defined series of steps in the process of finding a job.

> *Size does seem to count as more and more people gravitate to the larger sites which, not surprisingly, get the most hits.*

While the online experience may not result in connecting with an employer who invites you to a job interview, it should result in many other positive outcomes that can enhance your job search – from assessing your skills and abilities to acquiring tips on writing resumes, researching employers, networking, interviewing, and negotiating salary and benefits. It's an information-rich arena that should be fully exploited for enhancing your job search, which may be primarily conducted off line.

Given the continuing proliferation of employment-related websites, individuals face a daunting task of determining which sites can best assist them. Should you, for example, frequent the same sites most other job seekers and employers visit, or would you be better off striking out on your own and finding sites that best meet your particular needs, especially the many "boutique" or niche sites, or bypass the whole lot and go directly to employers' websites? Many people use search engines and directories to identify such websites, while others rely on periodic lists of the "Top 10," "Top 100," "best," or "most popular" sites as determined subjectively by self-appointed Internet or employment gurus or objectively by the number of "hits" each site receives. In the end, size does seem to count as more and more people gravitate to the larger sites which, not surprisingly, get the most hits. But if you follow such paths to locating the best of these websites, you may miss many small gems along the way. Worst of all, you may be on a very crowded highway involving high competition for low stakes. You may end up joining the growing chorus of frustrated online job seekers who discover that many employment sites basically function like classified print ads – generate lots of ad revenue from employers but result in few responses for job seekers. In other words, what works well for employers (accessing numerous resumes) does not necessary work well for job seekers (getting invited to job interviews).

More Than Just the Alphabet

Most examinations of Internet job sites, in either print or electronic form, use one of two approaches. The first approach primarily focuses on the process of using the Internet to find a job and is often designed for first-time users. Writers offering this approach include insights, advice, and tips on how to best use the Internet, with special reference to using search engines, posting resumes online, and sending email. They also include examples of major websites relevant to job seekers.

The second approach is more website-specific and results in producing a unique directory of employment websites. The primary focus here is to identify and annotate the best or top Internet employment sites. Writers using this approach usually provide an alphabetical listing of the largest and most popular websites – as measured by the number of visitors to the sites – which also may be cross-indexed by different classifications, such as occupation, industry, and job specialty. Individual sites are more or less annotated in terms of various user criteria – orientation, services, location, and costs. Since no one has evaluated such websites in terms of their effectiveness for either job seekers or employers, questions concerning outcomes are curiously absent or swept aside. Indeed, users are left with the impression, as well as an unwarranted assumption, that since these sites are large, popular, and featured by the writer, they are probably the most effective employment websites. Welcome to potentially disappointing and frustrating employment websites!

> *Using the Internet can be a great time waster – if you do not understand, nor stay focused on, what online activities are really important to your job search.*

Being Effective and Staying Focused

Throughout this book we focus primarily on the interests of the individual rather than on the needs of organizations. Cutting through a lot of the first generation "revolutionary" true-believer Internet hype, we've organized this book around the notion that Internet information should be easily accessible, purposeful, and effective. Furthermore, the Internet should play a role in, or be a part of, your overall job search. It should never be equated with the job search, nor play the primary role in finding a job. If you mainly rely on the Internet to find a job, you will most likely be disappointed with the results.

We make no claims about the effectiveness of any websites featured in this book. Anyone who does make such claims is probably greatly exaggerating the truth or only offers anecdotal evidence of effectiveness – presents "stories" or "testimonials" of success. We know, for example, that many job seekers and employers are disappointed with the results of the commercial employment websites. Fewer than 15 percent of job seekers actually find a job through such websites, and many employers no longer use the most popular websites because such sites have generated a low ROI (Return on Investment) for HR professionals. Rather, our goal is to make sure you use these sites to conduct your own effective job search, regardless of effectiveness claims of any particular site. As such, our central focus is on the **job search**, with employment websites being treated as **useful tools** for conducting a well organized job search.

We're especially concerned that you keep focused on what's really important in getting a job – following a step-by-step process that leads to desired outcomes. Above all, you should not waste valuable job search time engaged in Internet activities that have little or no payoff in terms of getting job interviews and offers, such as randomly clicking from one site to another or visiting numerous message boards to read about others' ineffective job searches or to receive amateur advice from self-appointed career experts. While such sites may look "cool" and appear "interesting," you may quickly discover there is much less available through these sites than what initially meets the eye. If you want to be effective, you must disengage from such random activities and become more focused and oriented to **outcomes**.

> *If you mainly rely on the Internet to find a job, you will most likely be disappointed with the results. It's all about conducting a well focused and effective job search.*

A Click and Stupid Approach

Like mass mailing hundreds of resumes and letters to employers, using the Internet in your job search can be a great time waster – if you do not understand, nor stay focused on, what online activities are really important to your job search. Devoting a great deal of time to conducting an Internet job search can quickly give you a false sense of making progress because you are putting in so much Internet time in on your job search. As you will quickly discover in using the Internet in your job search, motion with your mouse does not equate momentum with employers. Indeed, the frequent lament of many job seekers is that they spend so much time on the Internet looking for a job, but nothing ever happens. Forget for a moment what you're really supposed to be doing – generating invitations to job interviews – and your online job search may well be lost in cyberspace!

We understand the many promises and pitfalls of using the Internet in a job search. Not surprising, this electronic communication medium often gets confused with the message. Although the Internet promises to save time, generate information, and yield key contacts you might not acquire through other mediums, if not put in its proper perspective and used wisely, the Internet with its thousands of employment sites also can lead you down the wrong job search path with false hopes, dashed expectations, numerous distractions, and a great deal of wasted time.

> *Motion with your mouse does not equate momentum with employers.*

While we believe you must incorporate the Internet into your job search, we are not true believers in the efficacy of the Internet for finding a job. There are many different ways to find a job which do not involve the use of the Internet, especially through interpersonal networking involving the telephone and face-to-face meetings. Like a good resume, letter, or informational interview, the Internet can enhance your job search if you stay focused on what's really important. In the end, regardless of all your Internet job search activities, your next job may come from contacts unrelated to your Internet efforts. Be sure to use the Internet in your job search but do so with a healthy sense of skepticism.

A Focused Job Search Approach

Given our particular view of how the Internet should be integrated into an effective job search, we have chosen a **special directory approach** that is linked to a **process approach** for making better sense and use out of individual websites you will encounter. For us, incorporating the Internet into a job search is the old proverbial forest/tree dilemma: the job search is the forest and individual websites are a particular species of trees that make up one important segment of the larger forest.

Our first assumption is that most readers already know how to use the Internet. If not, they can quickly get started by using the resources identified in Chapter 2. Our second assumption is that most users do not know how to organize an effective job search. Failing to do first things first, like many users of Internet employment sites, most job seekers are often too quick to start their job search by writing a resume. Many of the large Internet employment sites, which primarily seek to increase the number of resumes in their databases as well as encourage more online traffic (advertising "eyeballs"), perpetuate a seriously flawed job search approach reminiscent of the traditional classified ad approach to finding a job. They encourage job seekers to post their resumes online before these individuals have a chance to do important preliminary job search work, such as assessment and research, for creating a powerful employer-centered resume. The result is often employment websites with lots of bells and whistles for people who do not know how to conduct an effective job search. The resumes that get entered into the databases or emailed to potential employers do not reflect the writer's major strengths.

Our approach is different. We examine websites that are most useful to job seekers in conducting an effective job search based upon a clear understanding of the job search process. Therefore, we've organized this book around key steps and issues in the job search process:

- assessment
- research
- networking
- resumes and letters
- interviews
- salary negotiations

We also include several other categories of websites that are essential to conducting an effective job search:

- education and training
- relocation
- career assistance
- employers
- occupations
- job seekers

As you will quickly see, the major employment websites tend to be preoccupied with connecting job seekers to employers through resume databases and job listings – our fourth job search step. Other steps in the job search process, especially the critical first step, assessment, are usually neglected or relegated to a few tips or advice from experts.

Structuring Benefits Around Eyeballs

As you incorporate the Internet in your job search, keep in mind how most major websites are structured and for whose benefit. Most sites are advertising operations that sell their services to employers and recruiters by "per thousand visitor rates" rather than by actual outcomes for end-users. Few, if any, websites are ideally designed to help the individual job seeker find his or her best job. In other words, they are not structured around the key elements in a successful job search. If they were, these sites would be designed very differently and with the best interests of the job seeker in mind. Instead, most employment websites are commercial operations that are designed around the interests of those who pay for these operations – employers. And employers have one basic interest in using such sites – hire the best quality candidates. Through a variety of user fees and advertising rates, employers finance these sites and thus largely determine the structure and content of the sites. Access to the typical employment website, for example, is free to job seekers who are encouraged to enter their resume into the site's database, browse job listings, and use other services provided by the site. Since you usually get what you pay for, the free services of these sites may not be very helpful. In other words, job seekers become the "eyeballs" for determining the number of "hits" the site receives. These "hits," in turn, determine how much the site will charge employers for advertising on the site. For example, a typical employment site will charge employers $200 to list a job vacancy and another $300 to search the site's resume database for a month. Not surprising, employment sites are primarily structured to maximize advertising and user revenue – they are designed to please employers who are trying to recruit needed talent at about one-third the cost of traditional print classified advertising. The services provided to job seekers – refreshed job listings, employment tips, message boards, company profiles, success stories – are largely designed to motivate them to frequently return to the site and thus increase the number of "hits" the site receives in order to justify the advertising rates and user fees charged to employers.

> *Few websites are ideally designed to help the individual job seeker find his or her best job. Most sites are designed for those who financially support the sites – employers.*

Given the basic economics of most major websites, few are structured with the job seeker's best interests in mind. They are designed for those who pay the bills – employers in search of talent to staff their operations. Consequently, it is up to you to determine how you will best conduct an effective job search by using these relatively biased employment websites.

Coming Up

The following chapters are organized around the interests of individual job seekers – how to best conduct an effective job search that goes beyond the employer-centered revenue models of most major websites. While we include many of the most popular employment websites, which primarily operate huge resume databases or job boards (Chapter 5), we also feature many other websites that fit into our model of an effective job search. Therefore, you'll find separate chapters on websites not normally covered in other Internet job books: career as-sessment, education and training, reloca-tion, and career counseling.

Always remember that your job search should direct your Internet activities – not vice versa!

Whatever you do, make sure you incorporate the Internet in your job search. But do so with a healthy sense of skepticism and with the knowledge that the Internet can be a valuable tool if used within the context of an effective job search. Don't just click around an alphabetical listing of the top employment websites. Instead, do first things first. Organize an effective job search that mines the Internet for key employment information. In other words, your job search should direct your Internet activities rather than the Internet directing your job search. If you do this, you will be well on your way to finding a job you do well and enjoy doing – one that is the perfect fit for pursuing a rewarding career. Better still, you'll fully use the power of the Internet to your advantage.

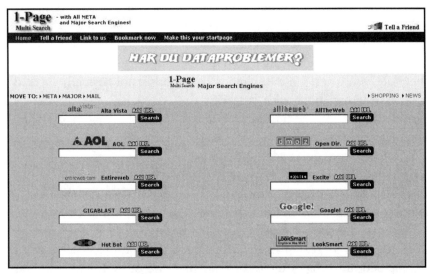

2

Getting Started in the Right Direction

USING THE INTERNET IN your job search is relatively easy and rewarding as long as you have the proper communication equipment, a willingness to learn, some basic organizational skills, an ability to stay focused, knowledge of what's most important, and time to explore the best of what the Internet has to offer job seekers. In the end, **time and focus** may be your greatest challenges, especially if you become addicted to the stimulating randomness of the Internet – a common affliction of many Internet users who spend lots of time going nowhere. Using the Internet wisely in your job search is what this book is all about.

Use Your Time Wisely

The Internet is an extremely seductive medium that can easily eat up hours of your time on activities that may have few if any discernable outcomes. Use your time, both online and offline, wisely since time is usually the scarcest resource in conducting an effective job search. In fact, we normally recommend that you spend no more than 30 percent of your job search time on the Internet. The other 70 percent should be focused on offline job search activities, such as testing, conducting research, compiling a portfolio, writing letters, and networking by telephone and in person. If, for example, you devote 30 hours a week to your job search, no more than 10 of those hours should be on the Internet; the other 20 hours should be on the telephone or literally in the streets meeting with important contacts and potential employers. If you find yourself spending more than 50 percent of your job search time on the Internet, you are probably wasting valuable time that could be better spent on other more grounded high-impact job search activities. In fact, you may be avoiding more challenging offline job search activities by hiding behind your computer screen! Whatever you do, don't forget the important social aspects of the job search and thus use the Internet to rationalize your lack of focus on what is really important to getting a job – making verbal contacts and meeting people face-to-face. As you may soon discover, the Internet can be a very deceptive and disappointing media if not used properly in reference to a well organized and smart job search.

> *We recommend spending no more than 30 percent of your job search time on the Internet.*

Basic Skills and Wisdom

Effective job seekers quickly discover they basically need to acquire two skills related to the Internet – (1) use search engines and (2) handle email. They also need to apply some **wisdom** to this process – know the promises and pitfalls of using the Internet in their job search and decipher which sites yield the most useful information, advice, and services. For the job search, the Internet is largely a search, retrieve, send, receive, and respond communication medium. Indeed, if there are only two things you learn about the Internet, make sure they relate to search engines and email.

Regardless of your level of technical expertise or computer experience, the Internet is very easy to learn, with most people requiring only a few minutes of basic orientation. Really savvy Internet users invest a great deal of time in learning relatively sophisticated organizational and communication techniques, from using search engines to organizing files and sending email.

If you are an Internet novice, or need to brush up on using the Internet, you may want to pick up some basic books, written in plain English, on how to use the Internet. You don't need anything complex, cute, or expensive. Get a book that goes over Internet basics, such as setting your homepage, bookmarking sites, saving and copying web pages, downloading files, using search engines, customizing web browsers, and using the Usenet, mailing lists, and email. Three good books that demystify the web with great brevity and clarity include:

> *The Rough Guide to the Internet*, Angus J. Kennedy (New York: The Rough Guides, 2003)

> *The Internet for Dummies*, 6th edition, John R. Levine, Carol Baroudi, and Margaret Levine Young (New York: John Wiley & Sons, 2002)

> *Sams Teach Yourself the Internet in 24 Hours*, Ned Snell (New York: Macmillan USA Publishing, 2002)

All three books complement each other. They represent some of the "best of the best" in Internet educational and self-directed texts. If you work through them step-by-step, within a few hours you should be up and running on the Internet with little difficulty.

Job seekers need to know how to use two things on the web – search engines and email.

For basic online guidance on how to best use the Internet – from dealing with subject indexes, search tools, email, and newsgroups to creating your own homepage and connecting to the Internet – visit these three beginner's guides and tutorials to using the Internet:

- **University of Albany**   http://library.albany.edu/internet/
- **Internet 101**   www.internet101.org
- **PBS**   www.pbs.org/uti/begin.html

Many city and county library websites, as well as college and university websites, also include a basic tutorial on how to use the Internet. In the case of colleges and universities, check out the library section of their site directory for such information.

A Library and An Orchestra

There are two organizational/disorganizational dimensions to the Internet worth noting as you prepare to use the Internet in your job search:

1. Specific locations: URLs (uniform resource locators)

2. Communities of interests: Usenet newsgroups, mailing lists, bulletin boards/forums, chat groups

Using a web browser, such as Internet Explorer, Netscape Navigator, or AOL's and MSN's built-in browsers, people go to the Internet to both find things (seek out specific locations by URL) and participate in discussions (join communities).

Imagine a library where millions of books are just thrown helter-skelter in one huge room. Or imagine an orchestra of amateur players without a director – where most participants are of questionable talent and are at times both in the orchestra and in the audience – trying to play a coherent tune or compose a score. In this chapter we'll examine the case of the library in need of classification, labeling, and location codes. In Chapter 3 we'll look at the case of the orchestra of amateurs without a director (virtual communities).

> *The Internet is like an orchestra of amateur players without a director who are trying to play a coherent tune or compose a score without knowing what their fellow players are up to.*

In the case of the library, nothing is labeled, classified, or indexed – even the covers are missing! While you may wander through the mess and serendipitously find an interesting resource, chances are you will be lost, confused, and frustrated about where to start and what you can expect to find along the way. You may just give up and decide this type of library is not for you. Without some form of organization and classification these millions of resources may be meaningless to you.

The Internet is like a huge library where few things have been classified and put on the shelves. In addition, it lacks objective gatekeepers who would normally assess the quality of information and recommend the inclusion or exclusion of resources. It's rich with information but chaotic in terms of organization and quality. While this book classifies employment sites and identifies specific resources by name and location (URL), the Internet also includes a variety of organizational elements – variously called search engines, search agents, and directories – that enable users to access resources in a relatively coherent manner. Not one, but hundreds of search engines, agents, and directories are available for exploring the Internet. Indeed, **GoGetTem** (www.gogettem. com) alone identifies over 2,600 search engines and specialty directories! The following sites also provide a wealth of information on hundreds of useful search engines and directories, which are usually classified by subject category or allow specific search inquiries:

- **All Search Engines**   www.allsearchengines.com
- **Search Engine Watch**   www.searchenginewatch.com/links
- **SearchEngineGuide**   www.searchengineguide.com/
  searchengines.html
- **SearchIQ**   www.zdnet.com/searchiq
- **Big Search Engine Index**   www.search-engine-index.co.uk
- **Skworm**   www.skworm.com
- **Infogrid**   www.infogrid.com
- **CUI W3 Search Engines**   http://cui.unige.ch/meta-index.html
- **DirectoryGuide**   www.siteowner.com/dgdefault.cfm
- **Search Engines Megalist**   www.search-engines-megalist.com
- **ICQ**   www.icq.com/directories

Creating a high level of redundancy, this multiplicity of search elements is extremely functional for anyone interested in accessing useful information on the Internet. The redundancy is often created by the fact that many search engines use the same databases (several use the Inktomi database system) and are powered by affiliate programs or parent companies which operate other search engines. Not surprisingly, a search conducted on one search engine may produce nearly identical results as the same search conducted using an ostensibly different search engine. While most of the sites identified in this discussion are often subsumed under the general category of "Search Engines," we've broken them into three categories of search elements:

- Search engines
- Search agents
- Directories

These are important distinctions because they can lead to different approaches to using the Internet and thus yield different qualities of information for enhancing your job search. In the end, your searches are only as good as the quality of your questions. The sooner you improve the quality of your questions, the sooner you will generate quality information on the Internet and more efficiently use your Internet job search time.

Once you begin using these various search elements, you'll start noticing some major differences in how you query various sites and how databases are organized and information presented. **Search engines**, for example, use software with "spiders" to literally crawl the Internet for keywords, phrases, addresses, and page titles that you specify should be part of your search. They basically index the Internet according to your specified search criteria. The "Big Two" search engines are currently **Google** (www.google.com) and **Yahoo** (www.yahoo.com).

On the other hand, **search agents** appear to be search engines but with one major difference – they explore various search engines simultaneously so that you get the benefit of multiple searches. Popular search agent sites, such as **Ask Jeeves** (www.ask.com) and **Dogpile** (www.dogpile.com), are often confused with search engines, such as Google and Yahoo.

Directories consist of compilations of websites, usually done by individuals, which are classified under a variety of subject headings. More targeted and judgmental than search engines and agents, directories typically identify the most popular sites relevant to a particular subject. Most directories include a search option, but this only searches the site's directory rather than the Internet as a whole.

When you use a search engine or search agent, you are basically asking a question, in the form of keywords and phases, for which you desire an answer. When you use a directory, you are presented with a list of sites, by subject category, with little relevance to any particular questions; directories merely expose you to lots of popular sites which may, in turn, raise questions in your mind. If you have many questions for which you seek answers, by all means perfect your keywords and phrases and use search engines and search agents. But if you're not sure what questions to ask, you may want to start with directories that expose you to many different related sites. After examining several sites in the directory, you should have a better idea of the types of questions you would like to ask of the search engines and search agents.

Please note that many search engines also incorporate elements of search agents and directories, and vice versa. In these cases, you should be aware that the search element functions very differently from the directory element.

Search Engines

An essential starting point for Internet users are the various search engines that enable them to literally explore millions of web pages for information relevant to their particular interests and queries. Entering keywords and phrases into a search engine's query form, the search engine quickly returns a list of "hits" based upon your defining criteria. If, for example, you're interested in finding a computer job in Seattle, you might enter "computer jobs in Seattle" in your favorite search engine in the hopes that you will get lots of good "hits" that will help you determine the best places to take that big leap.

Our Top Picks

Not all search engines are equal. Some have larger databases than others. Some use more sophisticated software than others. Some are much faster than others. And some are simply more intelligent and user-friendly than others. You may find, for example, that one search engine will only yield two references to computer jobs in Seattle whereas another search engine will give you over 20 such references. Since the quality and depth of various search engines differ, you are well advised to use more than one search engine when looking for resources on the Internet. Indeed, we regularly switch back and forth among five of our favorite search engines with often dramatically different results. Our current favorite is no-nonsense Google, which has proved very reliable and yields some of the best sites. A few of our other favorite search engines include Yahoo,

Teoma, AltaVista, AlltheWeb, and Lycos. Here are our top eight picks for search engines:

- **Google**   www.google.com
- **Yahoo!**   www.yahoo.com
- **AlltheWeb**   www.alltheweb.com
- **MSN Search**   http://search.msn.com
- **HotBot**   www.hotbot.com
- **AltaVista**   www.altavista.com
- **Lycos**   www.lycos.com
- **Teoma**   www.teoma.com

In our example of "computer jobs in Seattle," our favorite search engines yielded this estimated number of "hits" in a July 2003 search:

Google	350,000
Yahoo!	350,000
AlltheWeb	957,372
MSN Search	168,801
HotBot	124,704
AltaVista	101,606
Lycos	984,235
Teoma	78,800

The Most Popular Search Engines

You'll discover numerous other search engines for exploring the Internet. However, the most popular search engines should serve you well in your job search. Estimating 134 million active at-home and office users of the Internet, a Nielsen/NetRatings study conducted for SearchEngineWatch in January 2003 identified the following search engines as the most popular:

Search Engine	Percent Users	Searches per day (in millions)
Google	29.5	112
Yahoo!	28.9	42
MSN Search	27.6	32

- AOL Search   18.4   93
- Ask Jeeves   9.9   14
- Overture (GoTo)   4.8   5
- InfoSpace   4.5   7
- Netscape   4.4   4
- AltaVista   4.0   5
- Lycos   2.4   1
- EarthLink   2.0   3
- LookSmart   1.7   1

Emergence of Sponsored Links

The above rankings tend to be very volatile in today's highly competitive Internet business environment, which has witnessed the continuing consolidation of search engine firms and the rapid emergence of "sponsored links" (advertised sites) that increasingly fuel the financials of these business. In July 2003, for example, Overture (formerly GoTo), one of the leading search firms that pioneered "sponsored links" on search engines, was purchased by Yahoo in a move to create the ultimate search engine that would out-distance competing Google, MSN, and AOL. Ask Jeeves, which is more a search agent than a search engine (it also owns the search engine Teoma), emerged in early 2003 from near-bankruptcy to become a very viable company after discovering the enormous revenue value of "sponsored links." As a result, more and more search engines are moving in the direction of this new financial model – generating advertising revenue by positioning websites in "sponsored links" sections above or next to the more normal and "objective" web searches. Google is a good example of positioning "sponsored links" next to regular web searches. After conducting a search, look for the boxed sponsored links on the right side of your Google screen; they are advertisers whose business profile relates to your search interests. Sponsored links are paid for by advertisers who want to quickly appear at the top of any web searches.

Multiple Searches and Monitoring

Two of the best websites for simultaneously accessing over 30 search engines are the multiple search sites **1-Page Multi Search** (www.bjorgul. com) and **37.com** (www.37.com). They include the top search engines, search agents, and directories on a single screen for each access and multiple search. You may want to bookmark these sites and use them as your main search sites.

If you're interested in more information on the rapidly evolving world of search engines, be sure to check out these sites which regularly monitor the ups and downs of search engines as well as offer useful advice on how to best use them:

- **Search Engine Watch**   www.searchenginewatch.com
- **All Search Engines**   www.allsearchengines.com
- **Search Engines**   www.searchengines.com
- **The Spider's Apprentice** www.monash.com/spidap.html
- **Search Engine Showdown**   www.notess.com/search
- **Search Engine Ranking**   www.searchengineranking.com
- **Best Search Engines**   www.bsearchengines.com

Search Agents

Also known as searchbots, search agents basically search a few key search engines and directories simultaneously in response to search queries. These search agents are not equal since each conducts simultaneous searches using a different set of search engines and directories. For example, **MetaGopher** simultaneously searches seven major search engines: Yahoo, Spinks, Goto.com, HotBot, WebCrawler, Go Network, and AltaVista. **MetaCrawler** similarly searches the top search engines such as About, Ask Jeeves, FAST (AlltheWeb), FindWhat, LookSmart, and Overture. One of the stand-out sites, which requires downloading special software, is **Copernic**. Some of the most popular and useful search agents include:

- **DogPile**   www.dogpile.com
- **Ask Jeeves**   www.ask.com
- **Copernic**   www.copernic.com
- **MetaCrawler**   www.metacrawler.com
- **MetaGopher**   www.metagopher.com
- **Mamma**   www.mamma.com
- **ProFusion**   www.profusion.com
- **Vivisimo**   http://vivisimo.com
- **Search**   www.search.com

- Ixquick   www.ixquick.com
- HotBot   www.hotbot.com

Directories

Several sites that primarily function as search engines also include a directory section. This section includes a unique set of sites under specific subject headings, such as autos, cities, games, money, parenting, real estate, shopping, and travel. The real star directories here are About.com Open Directory Project, and Yahoo, which have reputations for compiling the most comprehensive listings of sites by subject matter. The major directory players on the Internet include:

- **Yahoo!**   www.yahoo.com
- **About.com**   http://about.com
- **Open Directory Project**   www.dmoz.org
- **Google**   www.google.com
- **DogPile**   www.dogpile.com
- **MSN**   http://search.msn.com
- **Excite**   www.excite.com
- **Lycos**   www.lycos.com
- **AltaVista**   www.altavista.com
- **Alexa**   www.alexa.com
- **Search AOL**   http://searchaol.com
- **Internet Public Library**   www.ipl.org
- **Librarians' Internet Index**   http://lii.org
- **WWW Virtual Library**   http://vlib.org/overview.html
- **Scout Report Archives**   http://scout.cs.wisc.edu/archives

Employment Site Comparisons and Ratings

While most web directories identify the most popular sites by category, other sites actually rank sites by popularity. However, it's not always clear what criteria was used in determining "popularity." Some rankings appear suspect (**100hot**, for example, is owned by InfoSpace and is linked to Overture, the pioneer of "sponsored links" on the Internet; **Alexa** is owned by Amazon.com), possibly influenced by paid advertising. Nonetheless, you may find such rankings useful in linking to specific employment sites. Be sure to keep in mind that "popularity" has nothing to do with "effectiveness." It just means many individuals are visiting such sites on a daily basis. Whether they get jobs from such frequent visitations is another question altogether, one that has yet to be addressed. Most website claims to "effectiveness" follows a suspect advertising model – the number of people who visit their site and access their pages.

If you're interested in the most popular job and employment sites, be sure to periodically visit these four sites, which provide monthly rankings of various employment-related websites:

- Alexa   www.alexa.com
- 100hot   www.100hot.com
- Ranks   www.ranks.com
- TopJobSites   www.topjobsites.com

In July 2003, Alexa ranked the following employment-related sites as the most popular by category:

General Sites

- Monster.com   www.monster.com
- CareerBuilder   www.careerbuilder.com
- HotJobs.com   www.hotjobs.com
- FligDog.com   www.flipdog.com
- America's Job Bank   www.jobsearch.org
- Net-Temps   www.net-temps.com
- Vault   www.vault.com
- Job.com   www.job.com
- NationJob   www.nationjob.com
- 4jobs.com   www.4jobs.com
- Employment911   www.employment911.com
- EmploymentGuide.com   www.employmentguide.com
- CareerBoard.com   www.careerboard.com
- TopUSAJobs.com   www.topusajobs.com
- DirectEmployers   www.directemployers.com
- WetFeet.com   www.wetfeet.com
- TrueCareers   www.truecareers.com
- CareerSite.com   www.careersite.com

- Snag A Job   www.snagajob.com
- Sologig.com   www.sologig.com
- BestJobsUSA.com   www.bestjobsusa.com
- SummerJobs.com   www.summerjobs.com
- Careermag.com   www.careermag.com
- LocalCareers.com   www.localcareers.com
- WorkLife.com   www.worklife.com
- CareerShop   www.careershop.com
- HireGate   www.hiregate.com
- Employment Spot   www.employmentspot.com
- GrooveJob.com   www.groovejob.com
- AmericanJobs.com   www.americanjobs.com
- Career.com   www.career.com
- 4Work   www.4work.com

College Sites

- CollegeGrad.com   www.collegegrad.com
- CampusCareerCenter   www.campuscareercenter.com
- NACElink   www.nacelink.com
- CollegeRecruiter   www.collegerecruiter.com
- Experience.com   www.experience.com
- CollegeJournal.com   www.collegejournal.com
- Gradunet   www.gradunet.co.uk
- CollegeCentral.com   www.collegecentral.com
- Jobpostings.net   www.jobpostings.net
- After College   www.aftercollege.com
- College Job Board   www.collegejobboard.com
- AboutJobs.com   www.aboutjobs.com
- Careerfair.com   www.careerfair.com

Executive Sites

- 6FigureJobs   www.6figurejobs.com
- CareerJournal.com   www.careerjournal.com
- ExecuNet   www.execunet.com
- ChiefMonster   www.chiefmonster.com
- Spencer Stuart Talent Nwk.   www.spencerstuart.com
- eKornFerry.com   www.ekornferry.com

- Netshare.com   www.netshare.com
- MBA-exchange.com   www.mba-exchange.com
- Futurestep   www.futurestep.com
- MBA Jungle   www.mbajungle.com

Industrial/Job Type Niches

- Dice.com   www.dice.com
- Jobsinthemoney   www.jobsinthemoney.com
- ComputerJobs.com   www.computerjobs.com
- Hcareers.com   www.hcareers.com
- CareerBank.com   www.careerbank.com
- JobsInLogistics.com   www.jobsinlogistics.com
- AllRetailJobs.com   www.allretailjobs.com
- HealthCareResource.com   www.healthcareresource.com
- ComputerWork.com   www.computerwork.com
- SalesHeads.com   www.salesheads.com
- Allnurses.com   www.allnurses.com
- Sales Jobs   www.salesjobs.com
- Absolutely Health Care   www.healthjobsusa.com
- NurseTown.com   www.nursetown.com
- Medzilla.com   www.medzilla.com
- Techies.com   www.techies.com
- Lawjobs.com   www.lawjobs.com
- Destiny Group   www.destinygrp.com
- EngineerJobs.com   www.engineerjobs.com
- JustTechJobs.com   www.justtechjobs.com
- Nursing Spectrum   www.nursingspectrum.com
- Legalstaff.com   www.legalstaff.com
- Jobs4HR   www.jobs4hr.com
- Nursing Center   www.nursingcenter.com
- Tech-Engine.com   www.tech-engine.com
- HireBio   www.hirebio.com
- BioView.com   www.bioview.com
- TVjobs.com   www.tvjobs.com
- AirlineCareer.com   www.airlinecareer.com

Diversity Sites

- LatPro   www.latpro.com
- DiversityInc.   www.diversityinc.com
- Hire Diversity   www.hirediversity.com
- IMDiversity.com   www.imdiversity.com

International Sites (English)

- Workopolis   www.workopolis.com
- Monster Canada   www.monster.ca
- SEEK   www.seek.com.au
- Monster UK   www.monster.co.uk
- Reed Executive   www.reed.co.uk
- Go Jobsite UK   www.gojobsite.co.uk
- Totaljobs.com   www.totaljobs.com
- Jobserve   www.jobserve.com
- Monster Australia   www.monster.com.au
- CareerOne   www.careerone.com.au
- Monster India   www.monsterindia.com
- Workthing   www.workthing.com
- PlanetRecruit   www.planetrecruit.com
- Nixers.com   www.nixers.com
- Gis-A-Job   www.jisajob.com
- Top Jobs   www.topjobs.co.uk
- Monster Ireland   www.monster.ie
- JobShark   www.jobshark.ca
- Stepstone   www.stepstone.com
- Jobnet   www.jobnet.com.au
- Doctorjob.com   www.doctorjob.com
- Jobpilot.com   www.jobpilot.com

Job seekers and recruiters are well advised to examine the latest annual edition of Gerry Crispin's and Mark Mehler's *CareerXroads* (MMC Group). While primarily designed for recruiters, the book includes useful information for job seekers, including several timely articles on how to effectively use the Internet – from online networking to posting an ASCII resume online – in one's job search. The book profiles 500 top Internet recruitment sites, which also serve as useful sites for job seekers who want to know where to post their resumes online and survey online job listings. It also indexes another 3,000 employment websites by a variety of categories, such as career management, colleges, corporate staffing, jobs and resumes, location, and industry. Updates can be found on the authors' website:

www.careerxroads.com

You may want to use *CareerXroads* in conjunction with this book, especially if you are interested in the larger universe of resume and recruitment sites, or what we often refer to as the "classifieds" on the Internet. Primarily designed for job seekers and organized around key job search steps, *America's Top Internet Job Sites* identifies the best websites for conducting an effective job search. In so doing, it includes several recruitment websites also found in *CareerXroads*. You can order this and several other Internet-related job search and recruitment books through Impact Publications by completing the order form at the end of this book or through the online bookstore: www.impactpublications.com.

Saving Time and Effort

Using the Internet in your job search can be a very laborious and disorienting experience if you primarily rely on search engines, search agents, directories, and listings for identifying useful job sites. While such organizational helpers are useful, they also can be very time consuming and produce disappointing results because of the hit-and-miss nature of such sites. At best these search approaches will identify the most popular sites in terms of the number of "hits" they receive on a daily basis. Such popularity may reflect more

> *Many exceptional quality sites, especially boutique or niche sites, may appear low on the standard search engines.*

on the size of a site's advertising budget, publicity efforts, and marketing prowess – by seeding their site with keywords and META tags – than on the actual quality and usefulness of the site's content.

In the pages that follow, we identify specific employment-related sites that we have found especially useful for conducting an effective job search. Many of these sites, especially boutique or niche sites, are of exceptional quality. Some may seldom appear, or they appear very low, on the standard search engines. You may want to sample these sites before venturing into the world of search engines, search agents, and directories. Indeed, you can save a great deal of time and effort by going directly to several of the gateway employment sites we identify in the next chapter. Once you locate quality sites, be sure to bookmark them and return to them often. In so doing, you may discover your time is better spent going directly to the special employment sites identified in subsequent chapters than in using the search engines, search agents, directories, and listings identified in this chapter.

Whatever your choices, you will at least be heading in the right direction for using the Internet to plan your job search rather than attempting to conduct an Internet job search!

3

Virtual Job and
Career Communities

THE INTERNET IS MUCH MORE than a collection of websites from which to access employment information and services. It's first of all a **community of individuals and organizations** that come together because of common interests, goals, and expected benefits. You use the search engines in Chapter 2, for example, because you are looking for something very specific, such as resume databases, a particular company, salary information, and career advice, or because you wish to explore new opportunities, from career fields to employers and job listings. In so doing, you may encounter individuals and organizations that can assist you. Hopefully you will make many new friends and gain useful advice along the way.

Information and Advice Communities

While most of this book focuses on the organizational players on the Internet – companies that have websites, staffs, commercial operations, and perhaps venture capital subsidizing their efforts – the Internet also is made up of thousands of individuals who have formed specialized communities that are focused on dispensing information and advice rather than conducting e-commerce. Most such communities are very loosely structured for exchanging information and advice. They are **virtual networks** designed for dispensing useful information, advice, and referrals. Some are linked to commercial websites, such as Monster.com, whereas others are independent nonprofit community websites or they reside elsewhere (Usenet) on the Internet. Individuals can easily join and leave such groups. Held together virtually by the Usenet and email, these communities are a mixed bag for job seekers. Some are very useful while many others are a dreadful waste of time. Some stay together for many months whereas others may only last a few weeks, depending on the quality of their participants and the benefits they dispense to their "members." Few such communities will last more than a couple of years.

> *These virtual communities are a mixed bag for job seekers. Some are very useful while others are a dreadful waste of time.*

You should be aware of your community options before you explore specific employment sites on the Internet. You will normally find three types of communities in three different places on the Internet:

- Usenet newsgroups/discussion forums
- Mailing lists or listservs
- Message boards of websites

While each of these communities has limitations, all potentially offer some very important employment information and advice. If you participate in these communities, you'll most likely come away with some very timely information – especially job search street smarts – that cannot be found from other sources on the Internet.

Usenet Newsgroups/Discussion Forums

If you are used to communicating with others by email, you know the importance and timeliness of such communication. Indeed, many people now have a hard time living without their email! At the same time, many people have discovered the communication advantages of newsgroups. Some become addicted to them – representing a unique combination of voyeurism and advice. User groups are especially popular with individuals in various computer and technical fields who organize around common interests related to particular hardware products (Apple, Mac), software programs (Linux, Oracle, AutoCAD), and programming languages (Java, C++, Delphi).

Newsgroups are one of the most interactive aspects of the Internet. Also known as Usenet, this is the virtual community aspect of the Internet – the largest electronic public discussion forum in the world. In fact, over 200,000 newsgroups currently function on the Internet. These are loose communities of shared interests where members or participants ask questions, share experiences, post alerts, review subjects, introduce new activities, spread gossip, and sometimes create mischief. Depending on the nature of the subject and the particular mix of participants, many of these groups are fun, educational, and exciting to join; others lack energy and are often boring, stressful, and useless. Newsgroups tend to live and die based upon the quality of the participants, ongoing communication dynamics, and benefits offered to the group. While not all of the so-called "news" of these groups is fit to print, some of it is useful. For job seekers, newsgroups can be very educational and timely, especially as networking forums for acquiring useful information, advice, and referrals.

Usenet newsgroups function as the largest electronic public discussion forum in the world – over 200,000 such groups operate on the Internet.

Similar to the many discussion and chat groups found on the major employment sites, newsgroups function like public bulletin boards. Someone posts a message which can be read by everyone who accesses the newsgroup. Viewers, in turn, post replies within the community for all to read or privately send an email to the individual who originally posted the message.

The Usenet is one section of the Internet, separate from the World Wide Web, which has its own networks, servers, and routers for handling newsgroups. In order to participate in newsgroups, you must have special software, called a newsreader, installed on your browser. Netscape Navigator and Microsoft Internet Explorer browsers come with this software pre-installed.

Newsgroups are an especially rich resource for individuals who wish to join communities of like-minded people with similar interests. Discover what they are talking about, including many of their major career concerns.

For information on how to best use newsgroups, as well as tips on which newsgroups might best meet your needs and how to create your own group, visit these useful sites:

- **Google**   www.groups.google.com
- **Topica**   www.topica.com
- **Yahoo!**   http://groups.yahoo.com
- **MSN**   http://groups.msn.com
- **Newzbot**   www.newzbot.com
- **Usenet Info Center**   www.ibiblio.org/usenet-i/home.html
- **FAQs**   www.faqs.org/faqs

Many of the sites include newsgroups focused on employment issues. Check them out to see if there is a group related to your interests. You also may want to create your own newsgroup and thus attract a group of individuals that will become a network for online discussion and advice focused on your career interests.

A good source for identifying more than 300 newsgroups relevant to conducting a job search is **AllJobSearch.com**:

www.alljobsearch.com

Also check out the **AIRS Directories**, which includes 190 newsgroups relevant to various occupational fields, resumes, entry-level positions, and general employment issues:

http://airsdirectory.com/directories/job_boards

You'll find several newsgroups on the Internet. However, you'll need a specialized search engine to find newsgroups related to your particular career interests. The largest and most popular such search engine is Google.com (www.groups.google.com).

Google   **Newsgroups**
www.groups.google.com

This is the granddaddy directory of newsgroups (was formerly DejaNews). It includes useful search engines for finding discussion groups by subject and name. For example, if you search for "Employment" under "Miscellaneous," you'll find the following relevant discussion forums:

misc.job

misc.jobs

Topica   **Newsgroups**
www.topica.com

This popular site is a major center for over 100,000 newsletters, mailing lists, and discussion groups. You can easily start your own newsletter or discussion group by following the easy online instructions. Like Google, Topica's search engine allows you to type in your interests and then it lists all relevant mailing lists. Type in "Jobs" and you'll get a listing of nearly 200 groups.

Yahoo!   **Newsgroups**
http://groups.yahoo.com

This is a well organized site for identifying relevant newsgroups. The search engine allows users to quickly locate groups with short summaries of each group and their total membership. If, for example, you search for "Jobs," over 5,000 groups are found in the Yahoo database – everything from Jobs for Comedians to Jobs in Bangalore, India.

```
┌─────────────────────────────────────────────────────┐
│ MSN                                    Newsgroups     │
│ http://groups.msn.com                                 │
└─────────────────────────────────────────────────────┘
```

This site includes thousands of groups. Look under the "Business" section for several categories of groups: Careers (1,783), Associations (1,433), Small Business (6,478), Companies (2,825) and Professions (2,439).

Mailing Lists or Listservs

Mailing lists or listservs are another useful way to access information and network on the Internet. Unlike spontaneous newsgroups that require you to take initiative in posting your own messages and/or checking on other publicly posted messages, mailing lists are more structured and are often moderated by the individual who initially created the list. Many are linked to professional associations. While most are open to the public, many also are private – only certain individuals who meet membership criteria can join. For a graphic understanding of how mailing lists work, visit this section of the Coollist site: www.coollist.com/tour/tour.cgi.

At the same time, mailing lists have the potential of automatically driving tons of email to your address. Indeed, with mailing lists you become a "member" or "subscriber" to the list by giving the group your email address. When messages are posted to the group, you automatically receive copies of the messages. Subscribe to a few active mailing lists and you may see a dramatic increase in your daily email volume. You'll no longer feel lonely with only receiving two or three messages a day – you could easily end up with 50 messages a day. After a while, you may think your membership is an exercise in self-directed spam!

The purpose of most mailing lists is to disseminate information and/or encourage the exchange of ideas amongst members who have a common interest in the same subject. Some lists are excellent forums for acquiring useful news and information, whereas others wander off the deep end as they generate lots of useless email from individuals who need to get a life. For example, if your passion is being a travel guidebook writer, a web designer, or an occupational health nurse, you should consider joining one of these relevant newsgroups found on Topica:

- Travel Guidebook Writers   www.topica.com/lists/tgw
- Web Designers   www.topica.com/lists/web-design
- Occupational Health Nurse   www.topica.com/lists/ohn

For a complete listing of current mailing lists and newsletters available through Topica, check out this URL:

www.topica.com/dir

The long-term viability of mailing lists depends on the quality of the information. Members tend to come and go ("subscribe"and "unsubscribe") by completing online subscription forms that officially put their email address into the mailing list. Many mailing lists become defunct because of the lack of time and interest on the part of the creator.

If you are interested in participating in mailing lists, a good starting point is **CataList**, which serves as a useful directory to more than 72,000 public lists out of more than 275,000 listservs:

www.lsoft.com/catalist.html

If you are interested in creating your own mailing list – which would be a great way to focus on a particular career – check out these four sites:

- **Coollist**   www.coollist.com
- **Google**   www.groups.google.com
- **Topica**   www.topica.com
- **Yahoo! Groups**   www.groups.yahoo.com

Using these sites, you can easily organize a free mailing list. For example, if you are graphic designer, you might want to create a mailing list that might attract many other graphic designers who have an interest in networking for information, advice, and referrals.

Because mailing lists have the potential of creating such high volumes of email, you may want to consider unsubscribing if you travel for a lengthy period of time. If not, you may be overwhelmed trying to sort through your email when you return from your trip. And you probably don't want to access such email while you are traveling since it can be very time consuming.

Message Boards of Websites

Message boards are similar to newsgroups but with one major exception – they are found on websites. Numerous employment websites include a community section which is variously called "community," "forum," "message board," "discussion group," or "chat group." Most are free-flowing forums (anyone asks and answers questions) whereas others may be periodically hosted by career experts. These sections enable visitors to ask questions in anticipation of receiving responses from other site users or hosts. In other words, these are **networking forums** for job search information, advice, and referrals. Most such message boards are relatively static – you must revisit the message board to look for replies. However, a few sites provide automatic email responses from message boards. In other words, if you leave a message, all responses will automatically appear on the message board as well as be routed to your email.

Some of the best, and most active, message boards for job seekers are found on Monster.com:

http://networking.monster.com/messageboards

We prefer the message boards of this website to the more general newsgroups and mailing lists because of Monster.com's large number of messages received for a variety of industrial fields – finance, health care, human resources, sales, and technology – and special interest groups – college students, management, women, and minorities. In fact, it's a good idea to survey several of the message boards to get a good "street sense" of today's job market and the many key issues facing actual job seekers, many of whom are frustrated with the whole job search process. For example, from reading the message boards in July 2003, individuals in IT and computer science were facing an extremely tough and depressing job market. Examining Monster.com's "Career Planning for College Students" and "Technology Careers" message boards can be a real eye-opener for individuals in IT and computer science as well as for graduating college students in general. Better still, you'll also learn about the many errors online job seekers make, including spending too much time behind a computer screen looking for a job and responding to message boards!

4

Gateway Employment Sites

EARCH ENGINES, SEARCH AGENTS, newsgroups, and mailing lists have their limitations when it comes to identifying key websites with useful employment information and services. Fortunately, several websites function as gateways for locating thousands of employment-related websites. They include specific websites for a variety of career fields as well as websites relevant to particular job or career interests and processes: careers, employee screening, executive search, freelance specialists, internships, job search, recruiters, resumes, and staffing services. The sites identified in this chapter outline the rich variety of websites available for job seekers. These sites literally function as gateways to the world of online jobs and employment.

Gateways As Website Directories

Many of the search engines identified in Chapter 2 include directory sections which list hundreds of thousands of websites by interest category. "Jobs," "Employment," and "Careers" are either separate categories or subsumed under "Business" or "Work and Money." Some of the same sites also include affiliate career centers and job boards for posting

resumes and searching for job vacancies. The directory sections of the following websites are well worth visiting:

➤ **Yahoo!** (Employment and Work)
http://dir.yahoo.com/Business_and_Economy/Employment_and_Work

➤ **About** (Careers)
http://home.about.com/careers/index.htm?PM=59_0222_T

➤ **Google** (Employment)
http://directory.google.com/Top/Business/Employment/

➤ **AltaVista** (Employment)
a/odp/us/?c=directory&s=job&topic=Top%2Business@2f
Employment&Partner=altavista_us_odp

➤ **AOL** (Employment)
search.aol.com/cat.adp?from=SEARCHHOME&id=71

➤ **MSN Search** (Work & Money)
http://search.msn.com/browse.aspx?ps=dp%3d%26m%3d
1082064%26&FORM=HP

➤ **Dmoz** (Employment)
http://dmoz.org/Business/Employment

➤ **Dogpile** (Employment): powered by InfoSpace
gpile/?c=directory&s=jobs&topic=Top%2fBusiness%2f
Employment&Partner=infospace_dogpile_dir

➤ **Hotbot** and **Lycos** (Employment)
http://dir.hotbot.lycos.com/Business/Employment
http://dir.lycos.com/Business/Employment

➤ **Excite** (Careers): powered by InfoSpace
dir.excite.com/d/search/p/excite/?foo=bar&c=directory&s=
careers&Partner=infospace_excite_dir

Several of the most popular web portals and search engines also offer career centers with information, advice, resume databases, and job boards. However, most are powered by a few of the major mega employment sites with which they have affiliate relationships. You may want to go directly to the mega employment site. For example, the following major portals and search engines have affiliate arrangements with the mega sites to power their employment sections:

Portals and/or Search Engines	Employment Section Powered By
Yahoo.com	www.hotjobs.com
MSN.com	www.monster.com
Netscape.com	www.monster.com
About.com	www.careerbuilder.com
Excite.com	www.careerbuilder.com
	www.net-temps.com
Dogpile	www.dice.com

Gateways With Wisdom and Judgment

Five of the best gateway sites primarily focus on compiling the most useful career resources for job seekers, employers, and recruiters. The first two sites are essentially gateway directories to job boards – websites that primarily offer searchable job postings and resume databases for employers. The remaining three sites are each operated by leading career specialists – Richard N. Bolles, Margaret F. Dikel, and Dr. Randall Hansen – who understand the job search process and who are primarily job seeker-oriented rather than employer-oriented. These gateway sites provide a refreshing balance to what is often "Internet hype" found on many other commercial employment websites. These are "must visit" sites for anyone planning to use the Internet in their job search. Each of the sites approaches the Internet differently, from many judgment calls of Richard N. Bolles to the huge number of career categories and linkages of Margaret F. Dikel and the useful content of Dr. Randall Hansen. It's well worth spending at least 30 minutes exploring each of these fine sites. You'll be a much wiser job seeker – both online and offline – for having done so. They will add one of the most important ingredients to your online job search efforts – **wisdom**! The other sites offer a huge range of recommended career resources for launching an online job search. Using these sites may simply overwhelm you with so many online career choices.

AIRS   Gateway
http://airsdirectory.com/jobboards

Wow! This is the mother lode of job boards and other employment services, the employer's guide to online recruitment resources. For job seekers, this site basically eliminates the need to mess with those print classified ads that appear in newspapers and trade journals. Here's the ultimate directory to the electronic classifieds, which include millions of job vacancies. Indeed, this site claims to have compiled the largest collection of job boards – over 6,500 – on the web. And they are probably correct. This is a wonderful gateway site if you are primarily interested in identifying electronic classifieds or "job boards" – sites that include lots of job postings. Designed for employers who are interested in posting jobs, the site also is a rich resource for job seekers who want to identify job boards in their particular occupational areas. The site includes hundreds of niche job boards that are often overlooked by job seekers. In addition to identifying 901 career hubs (general employment websites with job boards) in the United States, the site includes 330 international job boards, 1,325 industry job boards, 732 technical job boards, 305 health care job boards, and many others dealing with financial services (137), diversity (152), college and alumni (121), and free agents (86). The site also includes a search feature for locating job boards by name. You can easily spend hours playing around with this gateway site to the wonderful world of job boards. The site also goes beyond job boards by offering search services that cover more than 3 billion web pages in less than 10 seconds. This service allows users to identify people within companies, colleges, and organizations; search over 1,000 ISPs and web communities; and find gurus in newsgroups and mail list threads.

CareerXroads   Gateway
http://careerxroads.com

Brought to you by the authors of *CareerXroads* (Gerry Crispin and Mark Mehler – see our references on pages 25-26 and the order form at the end of this book), the annual directory to the best employment and recruitment websites, this site currently provides a searchable database to reviews of more than 2,585 job and resume websites. Three online searches cost $19.95 (the book, which identifies nearly 3,000 websites, is a much better deal at $26.95). The site is updated monthly with new sites and changes to the database. Primarily designed for employers and recruiters, who pay subscription fees to use the database, CareerXroads is one of the most focused groups for identifying and reviewing employment websites. If you are interested in identifying websites in particular disciplines or employment fields, this is the perfect gateway site.

Quintessential Careers   Gateway
http://quintcareers.com

Welcome to job search reality 101! This is not your typical flashy employment website with lots of job postings and a much hyped resume database run by inexperienced young techies operating with venture capital and naive concepts of careers and the job search. Run by career expert and author Dr. Randall Hansen, this is one of the richest websites for career information, advice, and linkages to the world of online employment. It's a smart site, because it's designed by a career professional who knows the key ingredients of an effective job search and who reflects this expertise in numerous sections throughout this user-friendly website. Well organized with the needs of the job seeker in mind (most commercial sites tend to be more employer-oriented because of their primary revenue stream – advertising), the site unfolds with a rich database of job search tools, articles, tips, advice, and linkages. It also offers inexpensive online career courses for individuals who can benefit from a more structured approach to finding a job: www.quintcareers.com/online_courses. Definitely the work of a career professional who understands the major ingredients – from self-assessment to negotiations – that go into conducting a successful job search.

The Riley Guide	Gateway
www.rileyguide.com	

Margaret Riley (now Margaret F. Dikel) is every job seeker's favorite online librarian – she knows where to find the good "stuff" and classifies it into many user-friendly categories. A relatively unadorned site, minus all the design talent behind the bells and whistles found on most commercial employment sites, The Riley Guide focuses on delivering useful content. This is Margaret's site, a testimonial to what one very persistent and focused person can really do to create a useful gateway site to employment information and services on the Internet. While it is by no means complete and is sometimes helter-skelter, this site attempts to be comprehensive and succeeds to a certain extent. For nearly 10 years, Margaret Dikel has led a one-person crusade to compile one of the largest databases of career resources available anywhere. The result has been "The Riley Guide," a major gateway to career resources on the Internet. Consisting of thousands of employment-relevant websites and articles organized by hundreds of useful categories, this site catalogs who is doing what on the Internet related to jobs and careers. It's not a fancy website with lots of functionality designed to stimulate one's desire for appealing colors, graphics, and interactivity. Instead, it's a bare bones site that delivers exactly what most job seekers need and want when they initially incorporate the Internet in their job search – lots of useful information and linkages about jobs and careers. Since the site is designed to "deliver the facts," you'll have to make your own judgments about the relative usefulness and value of the various sites and information that get cataloged in The Riley Guide. Many of the sites appearing on this website also are featured in Margaret F. Dikel's popular bi-annual Internet job search book, ***Guide to***

Internet Job Searching (see order form at the end of this book or online at www.impactpublications.com).

JobHuntersBible   **Gateway**
www.jobhuntersbible.com

This site is ostensibly linked to the author's (Richard N. Bolles) bestselling career guide, *What Color is Your Parachute*. But it does much more. It's a good gateway site to the Internet for one major reason: it's organized according to sound job search principles (begins with testing/assessment and proceeds to make critical judgments about the "do's" and "don'ts" of being an online player). Unlike other sites that merely present the "facts" – list websites, present articles, and offer job search services – this one performs the ultimate service. It has opinions and makes judgments about the good, the bad, and the ugly aspects of this online business. That's very refreshing since most job seekers don't have enough knowledge and experience to make good judgments about the quality and effectiveness of online employment information and services, nor do they have the bigger picture about both online and offline job search activities that lead to success. Indeed, like the author's book, this website has "attitude." Reflecting the experience of a career professional who knows what works, Bolles makes judgment calls about using the Internet in one's job search as well as assesses the usefulness of various websites. Many job seekers will find these to be very sound judgments – not just a sterile presentation of Internet sites and facts. After all, using the Internet to conduct a job search requires using good judgment. When you get frustrated by using the Internet in your job search – you see few results and often feel disoriented – be sure to return to this site to review some sage advice on why things do not always work according to expectations and why you are probably wasting a lot of time on useless Internet activities that have few if any payoffs. Not surprisingly, putting in job search time on the Internet probably has little relationship to making progress with your job search! This site tells you why this is so and what you really should be doing to make your time more productive. Much of this information also appears in the author's Internet job search book, *Job-Hunting on the Internet* (see the order form at the end of this book or order online at www.impactpublications.com).

Other Useful Gateways

The remaining eight gateway sites outlined in this section also pull together a wealth of job search and employment websites. Each uses a different approach to compiling its lists of recommended websites.

Job-Hunt	Gateway
www.job-hunt.org	

This site focuses on identifying the best job sites on the Internet. It includes tips on maintaining online privacy along with an annotated listing of employment super sites, job sites by location (U.S. and international) and career specialty, resume banks, employee sites, hot sites of the week, and several other types of websites. One of the best organized sites for locating websites relevant to different job search phases.

Career Resource	Gateway
careerresource.net	

Nothing fancy here – just hundreds of useful web resources linked to online commercial job databases, specific employers, professional associations, government agencies, university career services, alumni services, and other job resource indexes. A personal project of Jasmit Singh Kochhar, it was started in 1994 when he was a doctoral student at Rensselaer Polytechnic Institute. Since this is more of a hobby than a full-time job, the site is only occasionally updated (6-10 month gaps). While many of the links no longer function, there is plenty here to make this a worthwhile gateway career site.

Catapult   Gateway
www.jobweb.com/catapult

This is the resource section of the JobWeb site sponsored by NACE, the National Association of Colleges and Employers. Heavily oriented toward its university student audience, this site includes a listing of websites most relevant to its audience. It includes a comprehensive listing of university career offices in the United States, Canada, United Kingdom, and Australia. Many of these offices include rich databases of career information, advice, and linkages to useful employment-related websites, including alumni career services. Explore a few of the university career websites and you should learn a great deal about how college students seeking entry-level positions can conduct an effective online job search. One of our favorites is the College of William and Mary (http://staff.wm.edu/career/02/openindex.cfm), which emphasizes the effectiveness of their program. This site also includes a comprehensive listing, with linkages, of the major employment websites in the U.S. and abroad as well as many state and city career centers and employment offices and major websites specializing in particular career fields. A very rich selection of websites for directing your job search.

Careers.org   Gateway
www.careers.org

Discover hundreds of linkages to key career and employment websites directly from the front page of this useful website. Indeed, this is an in-your-face website with a rich selection of online career resources. It includes the top career websites, regional employment resources for both the U.S. and Canada, self-employment resources, career services, career advice, employer directories, learning resources, and much more. You can easily wile away hours exploring the major rich links found on this site.

This site includes thousands of online employment links with a greater emphasis on international resources, with particular emphasis on jobs for UK graduates. Covers career exploration, education, job hunting, regional and international work, self-employment, volunteerism, career fields, professional and trade associations, employer websites, and search engines. Includes many new links each month.

JobBoard.net   **Gateway**
www.jobboard.net

This site includes numerous links to Internet job boards and resume banks through both a keyword search engine and eight categories of links: general, business, technical, education, engineering, medical, health, and legal. By no means complete and somewhat dated, this site does include many of the major Internet employment sites.

5

Mega Employment Sites and Databases

SOME OF THE MOST FREQUENTLY visited websites are several mega employment sites. Highly integrated, extremely competitive, and usually organized around an employer-centered advertising and user-fee model, these websites operate like huge classified ad operations. Most are known as "general websites," because they appeal to all types of job seekers and employers rather than to any specific group. While some offer many useful services and features for job seekers – from message boards to job search tips and tests – their main purpose is to deliver recruitment services or "solutions" to employers and recruiters through large resume databases and searchable job postings. Primarily functioning as online recruitment sites structured to meet the hiring needs of employers and secondarily to assist job seekers in finding a job, these sites present a very traditional job search approach – managing job listings and resumes – that best serves the needs of their paying clients.

Managing Resumes, Job Boards, and Traffic

The central focus of the mega employment sites is the searchable resume database and job board. Without a large resume database and numerous job postings, these sites would not attract much operating cash. Financed by employers who post job listings, search resume databases, and/or advertise their company to job seekers through banners, buttons, and sponsored links – the three main employer-based financial streams supporting these sites – the primary goal of these sites is to attract a multitude of resumes and visitors ("eyeballs"), which in turn attract more and more paying customers, the employers and recruiters, who use these sites to screen candidates. The mega employment sites do a good job of attracting traffic to their sites because they offer numerous free peripheral services to job seekers. Finding new ways to sustain as well as attract more resumes and traffic is always a major challenge for these sites.

Old Print Wine in New Electronic Bottles

Despite all the fancy bells and whistles of the mega employment sites, the major job search and recruitment approach of these sites is very simple – connect employers and candidates by way of job listings and resumes. This is the highly formalized approach to finding jobs and recruiting candidates which was traditionally conducted through the classified ads in newspapers and magazines and personnel services of employment firms and headhunters. It's an approach that is useful for locating perhaps 25 to 50 percent of all job vacancies at any particular time.

> *The major approach of these sites is very simple – connect employers and candidates by way of job postings and resume databases.*

It's also an approach that leads to high competition for many uninspired jobs. If, for example, you anticipate making in excess of $100,000 a year, these sites may not be for you. Compared to classified ads and employment firms, one of the distinct advantages for employers in using such sites is the ability to search through and retrieve by "keywords" literally thousands of resumes found in a site's database. Two of the major advantages for job seekers are the ability to expose themselves, via their electronic resume, to hundreds of potential employers and to apply for jobs online.

How effective these sites are in helping candidates find the perfect job and assisting employers in locating the perfect candidate is another question altogether, one that has yet to be determined. For job seekers, these sites tend to encourage a traditional, and much flawed, job search approach: focus on your resume and respond to advertised job listings. Self-assessment, research, and networking – the real hard work of conducting an effective job search – are hardly evident on these mega sites, although some are slowly recognizing the importance of these additional elements and encouraging job seekers to include them in their overall job search by incorporating career experts and articles in a general resource section. Unfortunately, these sites may encourage job seekers to primarily focus their job search on using these sites rather than including them as one element in a larger job search. Indeed, such sites make the job search look quick and easy, which is not the case for most job seekers. In fact, many job seekers complain about the "ineffectiveness" of such sites: they get few, if any, "hits" that lead to job interviews and offers. If you primarily rely on such sites to find employers who might be interested in interviewing you for a job that really interests you, chances are

> *Many job seekers complain about the "ineffectiveness" of such sites: they get few, if any, "hits" that lead to job interviews and offers. Candidates with exotic hard-to-find skills and experience are most likely to benefit from these sites.*

you will be very disappointed. Employers usually have specific needs that are beyond the skill and experience levels of many online job seekers. Candidates with exotic hard-to-find skills and experience are most likely to benefit from these sites.

In the meantime, the mega employment sites are large forums for conducting the business of connecting candidates with employers. They are huge screening arenas that can be very cost effective for employers who normally recruit outside their own company websites. In fact, employers who used to spend $5,000 to $10,000 on classified ads and employment firms over a 30-day period to find candidates to interview may now only spend $200 to $2,000 to locate candidates online within minutes by posting job listings or searching an online resume database.

For many employers, these mega employment sites make economic sense because of the time and savings involved and the huge databases they can draw upon in searching for candidates. However, many employers also report that these sites tend to disproportionately attract job hoppers who are often more interested in playing the job search game (clever "keyword" writers) than in staying with an employer for more than 18 months. For job seekers, these sites make sense because they are free and offer the possibility of getting "hits" from a large range of potential employers. In other words, they are the ultimate free lunch – nothing to lose and perhaps lots to gain! For a new class of job hoppers, who get the 90-day itch, these are great places to explore new job and career opportunities – literally "test the waters" – 24 hours a day, even when they are ostensibly happily employed.

> The structure of these sites tends to be skewed toward the needs of the paying audience – employers in search of resumes for hiring candidates.

Welcome to the new world of traditional employment where speed and economics play a central role in the employment process. In the end, job seekers should never forget who pays for these sites – employers – and what they want – your resume. They get resumes through two costly methods: buy advertising (job postings, banner and/or button ads, and sponsored links) and pay monthly user fees (for accessing a site's resume database). Therefore, the structure of these sites tends to be skewed toward the needs of the paying audience in search of resumes from which to identify possible candidates for job interviews.

Structure and Process

The mega employment sites offer job seekers numerous free services that can assist them with their job search. These services also motivate job seekers to constantly revisit the sites and thereby contribute to the site's carefully monitored monthly "hit" or traffic statistics. A great deal of effort, including many subtle "tricks of the trade," goes into attracting high levels of traffic to these sites. After all, the number of monthly visitors is the major determinant for setting advertising rates and user fees for these sites. The magical word "free" now encompasses a host of enticing job search services, including free email alerts and newsletters, that hopefully will constantly bring traffic back to these sites so they can further sustain and expand their high level of traffic and associated revenue streams.

Once you begin exploring the mega employment sites, you may become disoriented by so many free choices available to you. But let's look at the real nuts and bolts of these sites – where things are supposed to happen for both job seekers and employers. At the heart of these sites are two major elements for connecting job seekers and employers and keeping the traffic flowing:

1. **Resume database:** Job seekers register and then enter their resume online. Employers pay user fees to access this database for finding candidates that match their search criteria. If all goes well for job seekers, the lucky ones will get emails or calls from employers who discovered their resume in the site's database. If all goes well for employers, they will draw on a rich database of qualified candidates who cost their company less than $1,000 to find – a tremendous savings over the costly, slow, and cumbersome classified ads and recruiter approach, which used to be the major approach of human resources departments.

2. **Job postings:** Like classified newspaper ads, most mega employment sites require employers to advertise in order to have their jobs listed online. Often grouped into "channels," these job postings are usually organized by job fields or categories. Job seekers can search for appropriate job listings by a variety of criteria, such as keywords, company, or location, and then apply online by sending a resume and letter by email, fax, or mail, depending on the site's application instructions.

Too Busy to Job Search?

For job seekers, the **resume database element** is the most passive way of finding a job. It's also the one element where your participation is required for the overall health of the site. Indeed, some websites pose this motivational question up front to entice job seekers to register: *"Too busy* *to job search?"* Just enter your resume in the database and wait for employers to contact you with an invitation to interview for a job. You can even update your resume on a regular basis. What a great way to find a job, 24 hours a day, and even while you are currently employed! This really makes the job search quick and easy – if you can maintain your privacy, get lots of "hits," and convert a few of those hits into job interviews.

Reality, however, is usually less than positive and often disappointing. Indeed, the experience of many job seekers is that they register and put their resume online but still do not get a single inquiry after 6, 8, or even 12 months. In addition to being frustrated, these somewhat naive job seekers switch over to the site's community forum section where they post a variation of this question: *"What am I doing wrong – I haven't gotten a single hit after being registered for six months?"* Not surprisingly, they get similar complaints from other frustrated online job seekers who have not received responses even after 8, 10, or 12 months! Thinking they may be doing something wrong, they review the "Career Tips" section or question an online "Career Expert" who invariably sends them to another section on the same website or recommends visiting other websites where they may experience similar online disappointments. The silver lining for the site is that traffic keeps coming back as job seekers repeatedly try to experience success. More traffic attracts more employers who pay higher advertising and user fees. The real winners are employers who manage to inexpensively find candidates through such sites. The experience for job seekers who use such sites for free is usually mixed – many get nothing.

> *The real winners are employers who manage to inexpensively find candidates through such sites. The experience for job seekers is usually mixed – many get what they pay for, which is nothing.*

Viewing Classifieds (Postings) Online

The **job posting element** requires job seekers to take a more proactive role in the online job search by periodically checking the latest listings in their particular career field. Some sites have even turned this element into a relatively passive activity by including a special email feature that automatically alerts the job seeker to new listings that fit their specific employment criteria. However, most of these sites require the email recipient to return to the site for information on how to apply for the position – an inconvenience for the job seeker but a clever way of increasing traffic for the site.

37 Peripheral Services and Features

Most mega employment sites include numerous peripheral services and features ostensibly designed to assist job seekers with their job search but which also serve as great traffic builders. You can usually expect to find some combination of the following 37 job search services and features on these sites:

- Job Search Tips
- Featured Articles
- Career Experts or Advisors
- Career Tool Kit
- Career Assessment Tests
- Community Forums
- Discussion or Chat Groups
- Message Boards
- Job Alert ("Push") Emails
- Company Research Centers
- Networking Forums
- Employment Newsfeeds
- Salary Calculators or Wizards
- Resume Management Center
- Resume and Cover Letter Advice
- Multimedia Resume Software
- Job Interview Practice
- Relocation Information
- Reference Check Checkers
- Employment or Career News
- Free Email for Privacy
- Success Stories
- Career Newsletter

The real value of these sites for most job seekers is found in the many useful peripheral services and features.

- Career Events
- Online Job Fairs
- Affiliate Sites
- Career Resources
- Featured Employers
- Polls and Surveys
- Contests
- Online Education and Training
- International Employment
- Talent Auction Centers
- Career Horoscopes
- Company Ads (buttons and banners)
- Sponsored Links
- Special Channels for Students, Executives, Freelancers, Military, and Other Groups

Some sites, such as Jobs.com offer a variety of PowerTools and Career Centers for enhancing one's job search. CareerShop includes a Personal Job Shopper service that generates weekly summaries of job matches related to their database. Such most of these services and features are free to job seekers, you are well advised to take advantage of such supports.

> *Our advice is to create <u>redundancy</u>: use all of these sites by putting your resume online, surveying the job postings, and exploring the many special services and features.*

Theoretically, the resume database and job posting elements together should make the job search relatively quick, easy, and inexpensive for both job seekers and employers. But the economics of operating such sites are more complicated than what initially appears to be a good idea. One of the big issues for employers and job seekers is the aging or "freshness" of resumes and job postings in a site's databases. Since sites try to maximize the number of resumes in their databases as well as the number of job postings – the two elements that make their sites appealing to both employers and job seekers – they often let the resumes and postings age beyond a safe two- to six-week period. Indeed, some databases may include resumes that are more than a year old. Sites that offer free job postings for employers may not automatically time-out the postings within a reasonable period of time. Consequently, some of the key data on these sites may be inaccurate or misleading.

In reality, employers are the primary beneficiaries since they quickly, easily, and inexpensively get what they want from such sites. Job seekers experience varying degrees of success and failure with posting their resumes and searching for job postings, similar to sending resumes and letters in response to classified ads in newspapers.

As you may quickly discover, the real value of these mega employment sites for most job seekers is found in the many peripheral services and features. In fact, reading the so-called "success stories" on the largest mega employment site – Monster.com – is very revealing in terms of what really works for online job seekers rather than what the site ideally wishes to publicize as evidence of its effectiveness:

http://forums.monster.com/forum.asp?forum+116

Indeed, you'll discover a wealth of free and fee-based job search information, advice, and services which can strengthen each stage of your job search. Our advice is to use all of these sites by putting your resume online, surveying the job postings, and exploring the many special services and features. If you do this, you'll create a high level of online job search **redundancy**. It's this redundancy that should prove useful as you include an online component in your overall job search.

The Top 10

Our top 10 mega employment sites are no secret – they are the largest and most frequently visited sites as measured by the number of unique visitors each month. They also are some of the most attractive sites for users who find them engaging, relatively easy to navigate, and useful for job search information and advice. They attract thousands of employers who regularly access their databases and list job openings on the sites. Monster.com, for example, includes over 400,000 job postings on its site. While most of these sites attempt to give some evidence of effectiveness, usually with a testimonial from successful job seekers and satisfied employers, almost all such evidence is anecdotal to attract more visitors and employers to the site. After all, these are advertising and user-fee driven sites where "effectiveness" is primarily measured as "inputs" rather than "outputs," and for good reason (most advertising companies religiously avoid questions about outcomes, which threaten their operations, and instead focus on the number of "users" or "eyeballs"). In this case, effectiveness is primarily measured by traffic numbers relevant to employers rather than the number of individual "hits" both job seekers and employers actually receive. However, one suspects something must be happening since so many people are hanging around these sites. For job seekers, that "something" may be all the peripheral job search services and features that both entertain and enlighten job seekers who feel they are making progress with their job search by visiting and revisiting these sites.

America's Job Bank   **Top Mega Site**
www.ajb.org

This site is the exception to the general rule – it's not a commercial website financed through advertising revenue. Rather, this is a mega public employment website operated with tax dollars and linked to thousands of local employment service providers. Don't miss this one since you've already paid for it. We're increasingly impressed with the evolution of this public employment site that provides a wealth of links to employers, educators, and resource centers, many of which are found within a few miles of your home. Our advice: start with this rich website before venturing into the commercial employment sites. Since this site is not driven by advertising dollars of employers nor subscription fees of users, the site offers a good overview of the most important ingredients that should go into an effective job search. This site offers the perfect mix of online and offline employment services. Brought to you by your government (U.S. Department of Labor in partnership with the states and private sector organizations), this site represents what was once an ambitious attempt to create a free nationwide job bank for both job seekers and employers. While it didn't quite work out that way, nonetheless, this site includes a huge database of over 1 million jobs, a resume database for posting your resume online (includes over 500,000 resumes), and lots of great resources for conducting an effective job search and advancing your career.

It includes a special Military Occupational Code finder for veterans. The site is linked to all public employment offices and career centers (One-Stop Career Centers, Workforce Development groups, Employment Offices, Job Services, Veterans Assistance Centers), and many commercial career services. Special features include state-by-state employment information and job listings, a career information center (America's CareerInfoNet) for decision-making, a training and educational center, and an employment and training service provider search center (America's Service Locator). Unlike many commercial sites which are primarily oriented to servicing employers who finance the sites, America's Job Bank is very job-seeker oriented with its emphasis on service providers. If, for example, you suddenly lose your job, just go to the service section of this site to find out what you need to do for assistance, from filing for unemployment compensation to attending job search workshops and getting one-on-one assistance in writing your resume. You can search for such free job services in your neighborhood by entering your zip code in the search engine. Often overlooked, this site is one of the best uses of taxpayers' money to help job seekers with their jobs and careers.

| **Monster.com** | **Top Mega Site** |
| **www.monster.com** | |

Awesome! Impressive! Fabulous traffic numbers. But perhaps overwhelming and too big to get noticed among the masses. For job seekers, it simply doesn't get better in terms of job search services, features, and job postings. There's more to this site than what appears on its pages. Indeed, for some reason the structure of the site has regressed during the past year – more and more difficult to access its pages. Boasting over 300,000 job postings and claiming nearly 3 million resumes in its database, Monster is the premier mega employment site. It includes a wealth of job search information and advice which is organized around several different interest and professional communities: administrative and support, finance, health care, HR, government and public service, sales, technology, college students, career changers, contract and temporary employees, minorities, and international job seekers.

From career articles, a newsletter, and a career assessment test to chats, message boards, resume and interview advice, salary calculator, relocation center, and bookstore, this site seems to have it all. You can easily spend hours exploring its many different sections. Claiming to be the world's leading career network, Monster operates a global network of employment sites in 15 other countries, including Australia, Belgium, Canada, Denmark, France, Hong Kong, Ireland, India, Italy, Netherlands, New Zealand, Singapore, Spain, and the United Kingdom. No other site in the world comes near the depth and breath of Monster. Many job seekers make sure they post their resumes on this site, register for its email notifications, and return to the site frequently to check out the various postings and services. The site is perfectly structured to ensure a daily parade of new and repeat visitors who add up to nearly 7 million unique visitors each month. That's a lot of people looking for jobs! Many employers understand such numbers and buy into this site accordingly.

Flipdog.com   **Top Mega Site**
www.flipdog.com

We really like this site because of its rich database and useful linkages to other career-related sites – definitely one of the best on the web. Indeed, this well organized site is a favorite of job seekers and employers alike who can explore a wealth of job search and recruitment resources through this one-stop portal. Unlike other sites that primarily compile job postings through paid advertising relationships, Flipdog literally crawls the web to find and compile job listings from employer websites – an excellent approach given the fact that more and more employers are listing job vacancies on their own websites rather than using the commercial job sites. As a result, this site can claim to have the most comprehensive directory of jobs on the web – five times more than most other sites. Boasting a large database of resumes and job postings, the site also includes many useful resources under its "Resource Center": salary information, employer databases (links to key employment research sites, such as hoovers.com and wetfeet.com), interviewing tips, networking sources, personal financial assistance, resume writing and relocation services, and career advice, tests, events, seminars, and training programs (through links with other sites). A rich site for exploring useful linkages to other career-relevant sites.

Direct Employers   **Top Mega Site**
www.directemployers.com

The brain child of one of Monster.com's original founders, this is the new and very aggressive guy on the block with a different approach to recruitment. Designed to challenge the standard commercial advertising model of most mega employment sites, such as Monster.com, Direct Employers is sponsored by a non-profit association of more than 100 major employers, including IBM, Honeywell, Bank One, H&R Block, Lockheed Martin, Merck, Sprint, Raytheon, Unisys, Xerox, GE, AOL Time Warner, Bertelsmann, Colgate-Palmolive, PacifiCare, Qwest, and The Vanguard Group. Members pay a yearly fee to both sponsor and access this one-stop recruitment site (and thus eliminate the need to use other commercial employment websites). Job seekers can enter their resume online as well as search more than 200,000 job postings and access job listings of the 100+ member companies. The site also includes links to numerous job search resources. College students benefit from the NACElink program developed with the National Association of Colleges and Employers.

HotJobs.com   **Top Mega Site**
http://hotjobs.yahoo.com

Noted for its aggressive marketing, HotJobs.com has become one of the most popular employment websites for both employers and job seekers. Acquired by Yahoo! in 2001, the site enables job seekers to search jobs by keyword, industry, and location. They also can target their search by salary and experience level. Individuals can view job postings by various career fields or "channels." The site also includes numerous useful career tools, such as a free email newsletter, communities (discussion groups), industry news, resume writing advice and services, education and training references, tests, salary information, interview advice, and general job search tips.

CareerBuilder.com   Top Mega Site
www.careerbuilder.com

This is one of the smartest sites on the Internet – very simple but loaded with great content and focus. It provides access to one of the largest databases of job postings – over 400,000. Acquired a few years ago by the Tribune and Knight Ridder and merged with CareerPath, CareerBuilder also powers the career sections of many other websites, and includes a branded Help Wanted section in many newspapers. A very user-friendly site, CareerBuilder's "Career Resources" section offers numerous useful job search tips and tools, including many vendors offering resume services, salary information, career assessment, continuing education, coaching/training, resume distribution services, executive recruiters, financial advice, and interview assistance. Includes a special hourly-paid job section that eliminates the need to apply for each job. Special features of this site include receiving job announcements via email, searching in Spanish, and conducting Canadian and international job searches.

4Work.com   Top Mega Site
www.4work.com

This is primarily a job posting service for employers. Rather than operate a resume database, 4Work offers a "Job Alert!" personal job search service that notifies job seekers when they qualify for particular jobs which are posted in the site's database. It currently has over 327,000 subscribers. This approach ostensibly saves both job seekers and employers a great deal of time because the employer-candidate "matches" are much more targeted. Job seekers also will find job search information and advice. 4Work also operates one of the largest volunteer and internship networks (over 107,000 registered) through its other website – 4laborsoflove.org.

NationJob — Top Mega Site
www.nationjob.com

Another favorite site for thousands of job seekers and employers. Primarily focuses on offering excellent job postings and a quality resume database. Its catchy "P.J. Scout" feature allows users to post their resumes, search for jobs, and sign up for job posting alerts by email. Includes a free email service for privacy and some success stories. Handles most peripheral career information, advice, and services through sponsored linkages to other commercial sites, including a free "teaser" assessment (through the same commercial linkage available on other employment websites, assessment.com); online degrees; company profiles; resume writing advice and services; reference checks; salary and relocation information; and success stories. Because of its sponsored-links, this site does not provide unique job search information and advice as you will find on several other mega employment sites.

Employment911 — Top Mega Site
www.employment911.com

Operating similar to FlipDog.com, this site functions as a one-stop job search and resume site. It searches over 100 major job sites which offer nearly 3 million job postings. It also includes its own resume database, which supposedly is accessed by thousands of employers, as well as its own job postings service. The "Career Tools" section includes many articles, stories, videos, and links to commercial job search services (resume blasting, online education, references – includes many of the same companies found on other sites). Special services for job seekers to manage their job search include free email for privacy, a free job search organizer, and a free personal web calendar.

CareerJournal — Top Mega Site
www.careerjournal.com

Operated by the *Wall Street Journal*, this site primarily focuses on executive, managerial, and professional positions. Individuals can search for job postings as well as use the "Job Agent" feature to receive job listings related to their interests. The site also is linked to related sites for college students, executive search, and international careers. In addition to operating the standard resume database and job postings, this site is rich with job search information and services: salary information, career news, job hunting advice, and tips for success. It also includes special sections with articles relating to all aspects of the job search as well as specialty sections on managing one's career, using executive recruiters, and dealing with HR issues. If you enjoy reading lots of articles on a wide range of job search and HR subjects, many of which come directly from the pages of the *Wall Street Journal*, this is one of the best employment sites to visit.

67 Additional Favorites

Several other employment websites also offer a wide variety of employment services, information, and advice. Most of these sites offer the obligatory resume database and job postings which are their revenue streams. Some offer extensive career resource and linkage sections (independent and sponsored). Our favorite sites include the following:

EmploymentGuide.com   **Mega Site**
www.employmentguide.com

Formerly known as CareerWeb, this site has increasingly become oriented toward technical jobs and community-based employment websites, with special emphasis on health care jobs and military and government links. This long-established site offers searchable resume and job posting databases. Owned by Landmark Communications and the Trader Publishing Company (yes, the publishers of the popular *Auto Trader* and owners of the Weather Channel), two major print media companies, the site includes featured employers and links to numerous job sites at the state level. It offers links to 55 of its local (city/metro) websites and to the many versions of its community-based employment print newspaper, *The Employment Guide* (over 3 million weekly circulation in major metropolitan areas across the United States). A resource section includes career advice and tips, an educational center, job fair advice and contacts, featured cities, work at home opportunities, and linkage to its specialty gateway website, www.healthcareer web.com. The Employment Guide is a good example of how to link community-based print media to electronic media in the employment field.

BestJobsUSA   **Mega Site**
www.bestjobsusa.com

Operated by Recourse Communications, Inc., an employment newspaper publisher (*Employment Review*) and job fair specialty group, this site includes hundreds of online job postings as well as a resume database of more than 300,000 candidates. Since there's much more to this site than what may initially appear on the front page, this site is well worth exploring for its many features. Includes many useful job search resources, from articles, job fairs, relocation (through www.realtor.com), and employment tips to the best places to live and work, career links, salary surveys, and America's top 500 employers. The site includes several state and local employment sites. Its "Best Jobs University" section includes career information and advice for college students. You also can view parts of the company's employment newspaper online. Combining both print and electronic media along with job fairs, this is one of the better sites for useful career tips, advice, and information.

Job Web   **Mega Site**
www.jobweb.com

Operated by NACE (National Association of Colleges and Employers), this site is specifically designed for college students and recent graduates. Its financial support primarily comes from companies interested in recruiting college graduates through member organizations – college career services or career centers. While this site does not operate a resume database nor post jobs for students – this is done through its new affiliate website www. nacelink.com (developed with DirectEmployers.com) – it does include a wealth of useful job search information and advice. This information is not always apparent given the current structure of the site. Its somewhat hard-to-find "Catapult" section (found under the "Career Development" section) includes a hot-linked list of college and university career offices, employment centers, online job search sites, relocation resources, assessment tools, job search guides, international resources, resume writing guide, graduate and professional schools, research centers, and international resources. The site also includes information on career fairs (online and off line), current job outlook for college graduates, employers, alumni networks, salaries, and publications (bookstore). Overall, this is one of the richest career information sites on the web with lots of useful tips, insights, and linkages not available on other websites. In fact, you can learn a great deal about conducting an effective job search by just exploring the hundreds of college career centers found in the Career Development/Catapult section:

www.jobweb.com/Career_Development/homepage.htm

Here's one of the best kept job search secrets few job seekers know: You may learn more about job finding by browsing through this section of the Jobweb site than by visiting all of the other sites outlined in this book! Many university and college career centers have developed extensive databases of information, advice, referrals, and linkages for anyone visiting their websites. Discover what career professionals at colleges and universities are doing to help their students and alumni achieve job search success. You'll be a much smarter job seeker for having visited the hundreds of websites linked to the JobWeb site through the Catapult section.

EmploymentSpot   **Mega Site**
www.employmentspot.com

A surprisingly well organized and useful one-stop site – one that makes more "sense" than most other employment websites in terms of issues and opportunities. Includes linkages to five "must-see" job-related websites. Offers job postings and a resume database along with a wealth of job search information, tips, and services through its linkages with other websites. Enables job seekers to search by location and job field. Includes three major sections that generate useful information and contacts: Reference Desk, Employment News, and StartSpot Network. Each section includes pull-down menus for further exploring key career topics. The Reference Desk includes one of the best organized and informative career advice/tip sections. The Employment News section generates numerous articles from a variety of print and electronic sources on what's happening in the employment field – a rich and comprehensive overview of topics and trends. StartSpot Network section takes you to related "Spot" websites. Offers a free monthly online employment newsletter.

WorkTree.com   **Mega Site**
www.worktree.com

One of the newer one-stop job search sites on the block (operating for more than three years), this fee-based site offers access to millions of jobs. Claiming to be "The largest job search portal in the world," this site offers linkages to over 50,000 job sites and career resources on the Internet. Members get unlimited access to a database of 7,000 recruiters, more than 3 million job listings, 100+ industry job sites, 100+ national job sites, state and local job sites, 30,000+ employer websites, and numerous government and international job sites. Members also can access the classifieds of hundreds of newspapers as well as the websites and job boards of the Fortune 1000. The site also offers free career e-books and discounted resume blasting services. Visitors can take a Quick Tour of the site prior to deciding whether to become a member. Membership fees range from $47 for three months to $67 for 12 months. Operates similarly to FlipDog and Employment911 but with a more systematic listing of employment websites.

CareerSite   **Mega Site**
www.careersite.com

This user-friendly site includes a quick job search feature with hundreds of job listings that primarily come from a large network of affiliated newspapers. Starred companies include company profiles which are found in CareerSite's database. Job seekers can create an anonymous profile to protect privacy, receive automatic notification of matching jobs, and apply for jobs online. A career resource section is linked to several content providers/vendors that offer everything from articles, online assessment, and books to salary and relocation advice. Closely associated with CareerLab. You may find this site appearing under several other website names or powering other employment websites.

| **Job.com** | **Mega Site** |
| **www.job.com** | |

This well organized site offers the usual resume postings, job listings, and career resources for both job seekers and employers. It also includes several specialty job search channels, such as information technology, sales and marketing, banking and finance, human resources, retail, executive and management, health care, science and engineering, administration and customer service, and supply and logistics. Its "PowerTools" and "Career Centers" sections offer job seekers numerous useful job search services.

| **JobFactory** | **Mega Site** |
| **www.jobfactory.com** | |

You can't go wrong with the wealth of information and connections found on this site, although some features and linkages are very dated. This is another powerful spider operation – its JobSpyder search engine allows job seekers to search millions of jobs across multiple job bases by job title and geographic area, and it links to over 40,000 employment sites with job postings. This site also reviews the top 250 career sites rated on a five-star scale; links to classified ads in over 1,000 newspapers in the United States, Canada, and 41 other countries around the world; includes nearly 4,000 hotlines with recorded job openings; and identifies over 5,000 recruiters with online job postings.

Vault.com   **Mega Site**
www.vault.com

Focusing primarily on company information, this popular site includes a wealth of career content and linkages for job seekers in addition to the obligatory resume database and job postings. Similar in many respects to WetFeet.com, with its emphasis on syndicating career content, Vault.com offers lots of career content for researching companies and organizing an effective job search. The site is rich with message boards, expert advice, salary information, career news, a student/campus center, and graduate degree center. Definitely worth visiting for the job search information and advice, which can be overwhelming at times.

WetFeet.com   **Mega Site**
www.wetfeet.com

Unlike most other mega employment sites, WetFeet.com does not operate a resume database. Instead, its primary focus is on searching for job postings and offering both job seekers and employers useful information and numerous services. WetFeet specializes in conducting research and publishing reports which are available for online purchase and syndication. It also creates several products and services to assist employers with recruitment and hiring. Job seekers use this site for researching companies, surveying salaries and benefits, and acquiring job search advice and tips from online discussion boards and articles. WetFeet's short proprietary "Insider Guides" to industries, companies, and job search skills are available as pricey downloadable e-books or print reports ($14.95 to $27.95). Employers can purchase an annual 110-page *Corporate Recruiting Websites* report for $1,995.00! The site also includes internship and international sections.

Net-Temps   Mega Site
www.net-temps.com

If you're interested in contract, temporary, or direct employment through a staffing agency, be sure to visit this site. It includes over 30,000 such jobs in its searchable databases. Most of the jobs are in the fields of accounting and finance, administrative and clerical, engineering, health care, legal, IT, management, marketing, and sales. Many of the jobs are for professionals and executives. Like other mega sites, this one permits job seekers to include their resumes in a resume database and search job postings online. The site includes numerous career resources and services as well as job search tips and a newsletter.

Jobs.com   Mega Site
www.jobs.com

Once a major employment website with its own unique content and communities, today Jobs.com merely links to the Monster.com and FlipDog.com websites – both owned by Monster.com. In many respects the front page of this mirror site is easier to navigate than Monster.com's front page.

Career.com   Mega Site
www.career.com

Not your traditional cluttered employment website with a very busy in-your-face, stretch-your-eyes, and scatter-your-mind front page design. Its clean and modern look is very user-friendly and focused. This is one of the web's oldest and most innovative online recruitment firms which has operated since 1993. Job seekers can search for job postings by companies, hot jobs (employers' critical jobs), keywords, locations, new grade-entry level, and disciplines. They also can save more than one version of their resume, transmit cover letters, and have job postings automatically emailed to them through a Job Surfer™ account. The site also includes a useful resource section for job seekers: articles, links to other sites, career advice, relocation resources, salary information, women's resources, college resources, career publications, frequently asked questions, and resume writing tips. All in all, a very good site that focuses on what this online employment process is all about – efficiently and effectively connecting employers to qualified job seekers.

Management Recruiters International   **Mega Site**
www.brilliantpeople.com

Designed for recruiting executive-level talent, this site claims to be the world's largest executive search and recruitment organization (Management Recruiters International) with more than 1,000 offices and 5,000 search professionals in North America, Europe, and Asia. This site includes a resume database, job postings, MRI recruiters, and an online resume editing and application tracking systems. Career assistance comes in the form of an online training center, articles relating to the job search, a salary wizard and relocation tools. If you see yourself as executive-level talent, you'll want to use this site to get your resume in the hands of recruiters who work with employer-clients.

Career Shop   **Mega Site**
www.careershop.com

This site includes three main features for job seekers – a resume database, job postings, and a Personal Job Shopper for automatically emailing job matches to candidates. Special features for job seekers include career advice, a career doctor (Dr. Randall Hansen who links advice to his fine gateway career site, www.quintcareers. com), web-based training (through MindLeaders.com), and a variety of commercial career resources (resume blasting, resume writing, assessment) through third party vendors.

JobTrak   **Mega Site**
www.jobtrak.com

Now part of the Monster.com online employment empire, this site is primarily targeted to college students and recent graduates –

those interested in entry-level positions and in need of financial assistance. As might be expected, it includes a great deal of information on making career decisions, developing an effective job search, and linking to the right networks. The site is connected to hundreds of college and university career centers and alumni groups. It includes a career guide that addresses various steps in the job search for college students, a major to career converter, salary center, internship checklist, resume center, and virtual interview. The site also includes chats and message boards which are integrated into the main Monster.com site. Its commercial section focuses on several financial issues affecting graduates – relocation, housing, mortgages, finance, insurance, auto purchases, credit, and shopping. Overall, a very focused site for college students and recent graduates.

JobBankUSA	Mega Site
www.jobbankusa.com	

This is a very user-friendly site. Job seekers can post their resumes online as well as search job postings and broadcast their resumes to nearly 14,000 possible employers and recruiters through a linkage with www.resumebroadcaster.com (not a free service). Its extensive career resource, news, and partners sections include Fortune 500 jobs, occupational guide, industry associations, hot companies, newsgroups, career fairs, assessment tools, relocation tools, career articles, resume samples, news sources, and links to partner sites. At times the site appears too eager to broadcast your resume for a fee – a job search approach of questionable effectiveness.

CareerTV	Mega Site
www.careertv.net	

This unique site offers a wealth of online resources for conducting an effective job search. Representing a merging of broadcast television with the Internet, the site includes streaming video television shows relating to companies and the job search. Job seekers also can search for job postings and submit resumes online, as well as explore several other career tools, through the site's linkage to www.careershop.com.

Jumbo Classifieds   **Mega Site**
www.jumboclassifieds.com

Nothing fancy about this site. Job seekers can quickly post their resumes on this site without opening an account as well as search hundreds of job postings. The search engine allows job seekers to search by industry, job category, location, zip code, job title, city, and salary. Not much else included on this site.

CareerExchange   **Mega Site**
www.careerexchange.com

Focusing on technical positions, this site includes a resume database for employer searches and job postings for job seekers. It also includes an online poll, job hunting tools (through reciprocal links with numerous other career-related sites).

Career Magazine   **Mega Site**
www.careermag.com

In addition to including the obligatory resume database for employers and job postings for job seekers, this site is rich with career resources to assist a wide range of job seekers, from students to executives. Resources come in the form of articles, videos, linkages to continuing education programs, free industry magazines, and lists of career events.

JobCenterUSA   **Mega Site**
www.jobcenter.com

Formerly known as EmployMax, this is primarily a job posting and resume database site. It claims to have over 5 million job seekers in its database. Job seekers can post their resumes and search for jobs online. The site is primarily designed for employers interested in searching its database and posting job vacancies. The site only permits job seekers who are deemed to be "Job or Project Seeking Professionals" to create online profiles.

CampusCareerCenter **Mega Site**
www.campuscareercenter.com

This popular website focuses on jobs and internships for college students and recent grads. We profile this site on page 216 – in the specialty section on college-related websites.

DICE **Mega Site**
www.dice.com

This is one of the largest and most important job boards for individuals in information technology. It includes thousands of job postings and a large searchable resume database. If you have a background in information technology, this should be one of the first sites you visit for information, advice, and job contacts.

ExecuNet **Mega Site**
www.execunet.com

Executive-level professionals expecting to earn over $100,000 a year find this membership-only site to be rich in job search content. It also offers opportunities to attend local networking events. We profile this site on pages 175-176.

Washington Post **Mega Site**
www.washingtonjobs.com

This is a good example of a community employment site that is rich in both jobs and job search content. It includes over 20,000 job postings and thousands of resumes in its database. Offers a message board, salary surveys, and information on local companies. One of the best designed sites on the Internet.

Other major employment sites which operate resume databases and/or job postings include the following:

- 6FigureJobs   www.sixfigurejobs.com
- Advance Careers   www.advancecareers.com
- AfterCollege   www.aftercollege.com
- American Jobs   www.americanjobs.com
- BrassRing   www.brassring.com
- CareerBuzz   www.careerbuzz.com
- Classifieds2000   www.classifieds2000.com
- ClearChannel   http://jobopps.net
- College Central Network   www.collegecentral.com
- CollegeRecruiter   www.collegerecruiter.com
- ComputerJobs   www.computerjobs.com
- Computerwork.com   www.computerwork.com
- Craig's List   www.craigslist.org
- Employers Online   www.employersonline.com
- Employment Wizard   www.employmentwizard.com
- Experience.com   www.experience.com
- Free Community   www.freecommunity.com
- GotAJob   www.gotajob.com
- Guru.com   www.guru.com
- HEALTHeCareers   www.healthecareers.com
- HireAbility   www.hireability.com
- HireStrategy   www.hirestrategy.com
- IMdiversity.com   www.imdiversity.com
- IT Careers   www.itcareers.com
- JobCircle   www.jobcircle.com
- Jobnet   www.jobnet.com
- JobStar   www.jobstar.org
- JobVillage   www.jobvillage.com
- LatPRO   www.latpro.com
- MedCAREERS   www.medcareers.com
- MedZilla   www.medzilla.com
- NACElink   www.nacelink.com
- Netshare   www.netshare.com
- Preferred Jobs   http://preferredjobs.com
- Prohire   http://prohire.com
- Recruit USA   www.recruitusa.com
- Recruiters Online Network   www.recruitersonline.com
- Saludos.com   www.saludos.com

- Science Careers   www.sciencecareers.com
- TrueCareers   www.truecareers.com
- Workopolis (Canada)   www.workopolis.com

While most of these sites are general employment sites, several sites also function as specialty employment and niche websites designed for such specialty occupational groups and job seekers as IT professionals (Dice, IT Careers, Computer Careers), medical professionals (MedCAREERS, MedZilla), college students (CollegeGrad, CampusCareerCenter, Campus Recruiter, College Central Network, NACElink), minorities (IMDiversity, LatPRO, Saludos.com), and executives (6Figure Jobs, ExecuNet, Net share). We review many of these and other specialty and niche sites in Chapters 14 and 15.

6

Assessment and
Testing Sites

W HILE MANY OF THE MEGA employment sites include
a self-assessment section under their "job tools" or "career
resources" sections, in most cases this is a very weak and
unenlightened section consisting of an entertaining interactive (self-scoring) quiz or a linkage to a commercial firm that sells career
tests and related instruments. Keep in mind that the employer-centered
financial structure of these sites has both intended and unintended
consequences for job seekers. As we noted earlier – but it's well worth
repeating – these sites are designed around an advertiser and user-fee
model (employer focus) rather than a career planning and counseling
model (job seeker focus). In other words, they are designed by advertisers
in collaboration with employers rather than by career professionals in
consultation with job seekers. They may or may not serve your best
interests, especially when it comes to the critical career assessment step
in a smartly organized job search.

The major goal of these sites is to get you to visit and revisit them –
initially post your resume and then return for surveying more job postings
or using online job search tools or resources, from news to message
boards. The more often you engage in these activities, the more "effective"

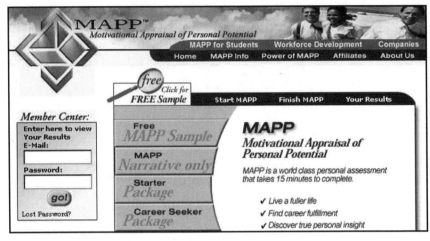

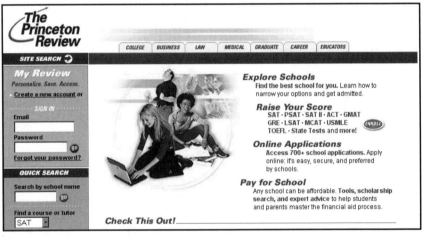

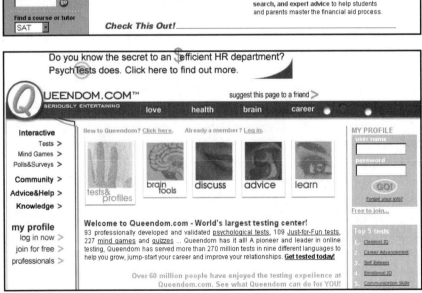

these sites become (higher traffic) in the eyes of employers who advertise and pay user fees to support these online operations. These sites are not designed to help you conduct an intelligent job search that would use the best career advice and instruments available. Just the contrary. They are "dumbed down" to get you to use their free services and to return to their site again and again.

Doing First Things First

Few employment websites deal seriously with what professional career counselors consider to be the key to career success for job seekers – knowing what you do well and enjoy doing. In fact, if the sites focused on what really works for job seekers, they would have to de-emphasize the role of job postings – to increase traffic – on their sites.

One major reason so many job seekers are disappointed with their online experience is because they fail to do first things first.

Let's play devil's advocate for a moment. One major reason we believe so many job seekers are disappointed with their online experience is because they fail to do first things first – just as they do when conducting an offline job search, but to an even greater extent online. Skipping over the critical first few steps of the job search, they literally plunge into the job search with a poorly constructed and focused resume, often encouraged by automated online resume database forms, that doesn't really reflect what they do well and enjoy doing. Worst of all, they are unclear what they want to do other than land a job that they hope will be rewarding. If they really knew what they wanted to do, based upon a professional assessment of their interest, skills, and abilities, many would probably start this process over again to find a more rewarding job focus. The online "click and explore" experience often further exacerbates what is a problem from the very start – the lack of focus.

But writing and distributing your resume via online resume databases and in response to listings found on job boards are things you should do only **after** you have had an opportunity to deal with career planning and job search **fundamentals**, such as conducting a self-assessment, formulating a clear objective, researching jobs and employers, and networking for information and advice. Rather than start your job search by posting your resume online or by searching and responding to job postings, you are well advised to do first things first. And the very first thing you should do in developing a powerful job search is to conduct a thorough self-assessment of your skills, abilities, interests, and values. You do this by **taking tests** which provide valuable information about who you really are, your values, and what you are most likely to do well and enjoy doing – your pattern of accomplishments. Armed with such information, you will be in a much better position to formulate a career objective and target your job search on particular jobs and employers with a powerful employer-centered resume that clearly reflects who you are and what you can do for the employer.

The most popular assessment instruments used by career professionals include the following:

- *Myers-Briggs Type Indicator®*
- *Strong Interest Inventory®*
- *Self-Directed Search*
- *Keirsey Character Sort*
- *Keirsey Temperament Sort*
- *The Birkman Method*
- *16PF Questionnaire®*

While most of these tests are best administered by career professionals trained in the interpretation of the results for individuals, a few sites provide online versions of these and other career tests. In some cases, you must contact a career professional online in order to use the instruments. Since these are important proprietary instruments, most involve a fee for taking and interpreting the tests. Unlike most mega employment sites, which offer a scattering of free online employment services to job seekers, many of the assessment sites charge user fees. As you will quickly discover, many of these powerful assessment instruments are well worth the price, especially since they can change the direction of your job search by putting you on a more productive path. Once you discover what it is you do well and enjoy doing, you'll be prepared to develop a well focused resume designed to clearly communicate who you are, what you can do, and what you want to do in the future. Best of all, you should be better prepared to handle the most important phase of the job search process –

the job interview. For in the end, the whole purpose of the job search, whether conducted online or offline, is to get job interviews that result in job offers.

If you fail to do first things first, you will most likely wander in the job market looking for jobs that appear interesting and which you think you might be able to fit into. Your goals should be to find a job that is fit for you, one that is compatible with your values and past patterns of behavior.

Beware of 21st Century Snake Oil

At the same time, one should also approach these testing and assessment approaches with a critical eye. Many of them still use 19th and early 20th century typological classifications and analyses, which sometimes border on being a form of 21st century scientific snake oil. Indeed, many career counselors prefer using self-directed assessment approaches to many of the professionally administered assessment instruments. At the same time, many of these tests tend to be under-whelming, because they often discover the obvious, which results in a temporary "Aha" response from job seekers who recognize in writing what they already know intuitively about themselves. In the end, a positive thinking and motivational approach – setting clear goals and pursuing them with passion – may be more useful to achieving career success than all the introspective data generated on "understanding" yourself and charting a course of action based on your past patterns of motivation and behavior.

Online Assessments

Several sites specialize in providing career testing and assessment services. While you can easily and inexpensively acquire such services through your local community or junior college or through a professional testing and assessment center (you also may want to contact your nearest public employment office or career center by searching through America's Job Bank database: www.ajb.org), you may want to examine several of the following sites for acquiring these services online, or at least familiarize yourself with several important testing alternatives. If you enjoy taking self-assessment tests to probe your "inner self," you'll love many of the sites outlined in the remainder of this chapter. If you are a "test junkie," you'll probably spend many hours exploring the many recommended websites in this chapter! Some of the sites featured here offer relatively sophisticated fee-based tests whereas others offer free sample tests and quizzes. All of these sites are worth visiting just to discover what you should probably be doing, first.

MAPP   Assessment
www.assessment.com

You can't miss this firm online since it has developed affiliate partnerships with several employment websites that directly link to this site as part of a revenue-sharing relationship. Known as MAPP (Motivational Appraisal of Personal Potential), this company offers a free online career analysis for sampling their assessment instruments. It also offers a variety of products in the form of assessment appraisals, profiles, and reports that focus on motivation and career interests: Student Appraisal, Career Appraisal, Personal Appraisal, and a MAPP Match™ for individuals. The MAPP Match™, for example, helps individuals explore different jobs and careers by matching their test results with over 900 jobs in the U.S. Department of Labor's O*NET database and generating a 15-20 page narrative report. The cost is $19.95, but the firm often runs online specials for $9.95. It offers other packages – Career Seeker and Executive – that cost from $39.95 to $129.95. This company understands career planning and job search fundamentals when it states on its site that "Assessment testing is the first step to establish the learner's strengths and career goals." The site has expanded its testing offerings to help students (K-12) "get better grades, pick the right major, and find jobs they enjoy." Most assessments take only 15 minutes to complete. The results can have a dramatic affect on how you organize your job search and communicate qualifications to employers. MAPP could become your one-stop shop for career testing. However, be sure to check out many of the remaining assessment websites in this chapter before committing yourself to the assessment instruments available through this site.

Keirsey Character Sorter and   **Assessment**
Keirsey Temperament Sorter   **Keirsey Instruments**
www.keirsey.com

Based on the *Myers-Briggs Type Indicator®* and Dr. Kersey's two
bestselling books, ***Please Understand Me*** and ***Please Understand
Me II***, the Keirsey temperament approach classifies individuals
into four temperaments: Guardian, Artisan, Idealist, and Rational.
This site provides detailed information on these two assessment
devices, including questions and answers, as well as contrasts the
Keirsey approach with what they see as the less stable results of
the *Myers-Briggs Type Indicator®*. The site offers online question-
naires for taking tests in English, Spanish, French, Portuguese,
German, Norwegian, Swedish, Bosnian, Czech, Polish, Russian,
Finnish, Ukrainian, Danish, and Japanese. It also includes recommended resources related to the Keirsey approach.

PersonalityType   **Assessment**
www.personalitytype.com   **Type**

This is the website of psychologists and bestselling authors Paul D.
Tieger and Barbara Barron-Tieger (*Do What You Are*, *Nurture By
Nature*, *The Art of Speedreading People*, and *Just Your Type*).
Using the popular personality type approach (based on the *Myers-
Briggs Type Indicator®* and a whole school of "Type" psychologists
who provide answers to all kinds of life challenges through their
typological analyses), they offer an online quiz to help you identify
your "Type." They claim this information will help you better deal
with your career, love life, parenting skills, and communication
with others – like a key to unlocking all of life's problems. The site
includes linkages to professional organizations and Type experts as
well as FAQs, a store, their books, and other resources.

Personality Online   **Assessment**
www.personalityonline.com

This inviting site will really help you probe various dimensions of
your personality. It includes nine self-scoring personality tests as

well as information on analysis and resources relating to personal development. Several of the tests have implications for career decision-making: Keirsey Temperament Sorter, The Enneagram, Personality Profile, The Geek Test, The Nerd Test, and the Maykorner Test. The site also includes a few fun tests: The Love Test, The Colour Test, and The Purity Test. The site is especially noted for the Enneagram, a popular self-discovery device, which measures personality along nine different scales and which are linked to several personality traits; it includes 180 questions, resulting in the user being classified into nine different types: Perfectionist, Giver, Performer, Tragic Romantic, Observer, Devil's Advocate, Epicure, Boss, and Mediator (for more information on the Enneagram, visit www.ennea.com). The 80-statement Personality Profile measures users on 14 different profiles or "types" which are related to personality traits.

Self-Directed Search   Assessment
www.self-directed-search.com

This is the home site for John Holland's popular *Self-Directed Search (SDS)* which is used by millions of students and job seekers each year. The SDS classifies individuals into six categories: Realistic, Investigative, Artistic, Social, Enterprising, and Conventional. A proprietary self-assessment device produced by Psychological Assessment Resources (PAR), the SDS has influenced the thinking of many career counselors and is the basis for much of Richard Bolles's self-assessment devices, including his popular *Quick Job Hunting Map*. This site explains the SDS and provides an example of an SDS report for someone with an ESC Holland code. Visitors to this site can take a 15-minute online version of the SDS and have the results printed out (8-12 page report) for $8.95 (takes credit cards online). The site also includes information on selecting a career counselor, along with linkages to the National Career Development Association (www.ncda.org) and the National Board of Certified Counselors (www.nbcc.org).

The Princeton Review Career Quiz   Assessment
Performance Profile Survey (Birkman Method)
www.princetonreview.com/cte/quiz/quizoverview.asp

These two self-assessment instruments are administered on the Princeton Review site through Strategic Solutions International, Inc. (www.ssicareerzone.com). *The Princeton Review Career Quiz* is a 24-question quiz designed to help users determine their most likely interests and work style for making better career choices. After registering and taking this free online quiz, you receive lots of information on jobs and careers relating to the analysis of your answers. Much of the same information is found in the book, ***The Princeton Review Guide to Your Career***. The *Performance Profile Survey* is based on The Birkman Method, a popular "psychometric" tool used by thousands of companies and organizations each year to measure human characteristics and behavior to determine what motivates individuals and how they handle stress and how well they deal with others. It takes about 40 minutes to complete this survey. The end result is a "SSI Profile" that gives the user a strong understanding of who they are as a person and which jobs they would most likely be good at. The online *Performance Profile Survey* costs from $39.95 to $49.95, depending on whether or not SSI is running a sale. Both online instruments often generate surprising results for both job seekers and career counselors.

Analyze My Career   Assessment
www.analyzemycareer.com

This site offers numerous tests and assessment devices for job seekers through its Test Center – aptitude, personality, occupational interest, and entrepreneurial index. It also includes a "suite" – an integrated report called "Expert Opinion." While this site includes a free sample section, most tests are fee-based, with prices ranging from $19.95 to $49.95. This is an excellent one-stop shop for meeting several testing needs.

U.S. Department of Interior   Assessment
www.doi.gov/octc/typescar.html   MBTI Career Chart

For a good example of how the *Myers-Briggs Type Indicator*® relates to specific jobs and careers (without having to take the test) visit this useful page, which includes 16 personality types with corresponding jobs and careers linked to each. If, for example, you are an ISTJ type, chances are you will enjoy being an engineer, stock broker, police officer, or real estate agent.

Career Services Group   Assessment
www.careerperfect.com

Offers information and advice on various types of career inventories and tests: career interest, values, skills, and personality. Includes a self-scored "Work Preference Inventory." Also includes four software programs which can be purchased through the site's store: *CareerDesign*™ ($49.95), *My Personal Profile*™ ($17.95), *The Right Job*™ ($34.95), and *InterviewSmart*™ ($29.95). Check out other sections of this site for several additional job search services, from resume writing and distribution to interview advice and salary surveys.

Personality and IQ Tests   Assessment
www.davideck.com

Test junkies will love this aggregate site. It's jam-packed with linkages to a variety of personality, IQ, love, health, career, and other fun tests. Each test is rated on a scale of 0 to 4. The personality test section includes the IPIP-NEO (competitor to the *Myers-Briggs Type Indicator*®), Enneagram, Kingdomality Personality, Keirsey Temperament, Goofy Personality, and more than 20 other tests. The IQ test section includes 22 different tests to measure one's IQ. The career test section includes the following tests and quizzes: Time Management, Business Etiquette, Ace the Interview, Handling Difficult Workers, Typing, Entrepreneur, Career Analysis, Hard Work, Income, Success Indicator, Efficient or Effective,

Interdependence, Lifelong Learning, Partnering Skills, Super Achiever, Job Change, Work and Play, Being a Boss, Dealing With Bosses, and The Princeton Review Career Quiz. Other fun tests include the QueenDom Communication Skills Inventory and the Weirdness Test. A very revealing test site!

QueenDom **Assessment**
www.queendom.com

This website has come a long way in the past two years. Calling itself "seriously entertaining," QueenDom seems to have it all under one cyber roof. Test junkies also will enjoy exploring this rich testing site. It currently includes 93 psychological tests, 109 just-for-fun tests, and 227 mind games and quizzes. Its five most popular tests are the Classical Intelligence, Career Advancement, Self Esteem, Emotional IQ, and Communication Skills. A career test section includes 19 tests that focus on several important employment subjects and issues: anger, assertiveness, burnout, career concentration, coping skills, goal setting, intelligence, leadership, management type, power profile, perfectionism, procrastination, resilience, likely success, sales personality, and time management. The site also includes discussion boards, counseling referrals, and expert advice.

Tests on the Web **Assessment**
www.2h.com

This bare-bones site includes a variety of IQ, personality, and entrepreneurial tests available though linkages with other websites, such as AnalyzeMyCareer.com. The tests are listed by title and accompanied by a short description and the amount of time to complete each one. The personality test section, for example, includes five tests: Color Quiz, Career Values Inventory, Ansir, Kersey Temperament Sorter, and VALS.

Fortune.com   Assessment
www.fortune.com/fortune/careers

Fortune magazine's website offers seven free quizzes for employees and job seekers:

- *Do You Deserve a Raise?*
- *How Stressed Are You?*
- *What's the Right Work-Life Balance Strategy for You?*
- *Do You Have a Fear of Success?*
- *What's Your EQ At Work?*
- *Will I Get Promoted Soon?*
- *Could You Make It to CEO?*

Profiler   Assessment
www.profiler.com

Offers an online version of the popular CISS (Campbell™ Interest and Skill Survey) assessment to help job seekers discover their right fit in the world of work. The CISS report compares test results with people who are successfully employed in the same fields. Costing $17.95, the personalized report covers nearly 60 occupations and includes a comprehensive career planner for interpreting results.

CareerLab.com   Assessment
www.careerlab.com

Operated by career advisor and author William S. Frank and his team, this site specializes in career assessment and related career services for professionals. It primarily uses *The Birkman Method* (includes a good description of this powerful assessment tool), although it occasionally will use other assessment tools, such as

- *Campbell Interest and Skill Survey (CISS)*
- *Myers-Briggs Type Indicator (MBTI)*
- *16PF Questionnaire®*

- *California Psychological Inventory (CPI)*
- *Campbell Leadership Index*

The site also includes useful articles, consulting services, networking opportunities, and other corporate-related services.

College Board   **Assessment**
www.myroad.com

Presented by the College Board, the tests offered on this specialty site under the "I.D. Me" section help students get a better understanding of themselves for planning their college and career. Includes career assessments, personality type, *QuickStarts*, and the *ORA Personality Profiler*. Individuals must register in order to use this site. Before doing so, take a tour of the site to find out what it's all about. Designed for exploring college and career options.

CareerLeader™   **Assessment**
www.careerdiscovery.com/careerleader

CareerLeader™ is a comprehensive business career development tool designed to help individuals discover their best career in business and thus better focus their job search. Developed by Drs. James Waldroop and Timothy Butler, directors of MBA Career Development Programs at Harvard Business School, it's an interactive, online program used by over 120 top business and MBA programs in the U.S. and Europe to guide students and help companies retain employees. It includes three inventories that focus on business-relevant interests, values, and abilities to help individuals with their business careers: *Business Career Interest Inventory, Management and Professional Rewards Profile,* and *Management and Professional Abilities Profile.* The resulting profiles recommend the best career path matches. Costs $95.00 for a 60-day online access membership and comes with a full money-back guarantee within seven days of purchase.

Careers By Design®   Assessment
www.careers-by-design.com

This company offers four popular assessment devices online followed by telephone counseling sessions for interpreting results:

- *Strong Interest Inventory®*
- *Myers-Briggs Type Indicator®*
- *FIRO-B™*
- *16PF Questionnaire®*

The site offers summary explanations of each instrument in order to help users understand which ones might be most appropriate for their needs. This section alone is worth visiting the site, especially if you're new to this assessment business. Each assessment instruments costs from $50.00 to $75.00 for individuals, depending on the product.

My Future   Assessment
www.myfuture.com

This site includes a *Work Interest Quiz* and a *Personality Test* in its "Career Toolbox" section. The Work Interest Quiz, which is both quick and free, is a modified version of Dr. John Holland's *Self-Directed Search*. It helps users answer these questions: Should I go to college or look for a job? If I try to find a job, what kind of job should it be? How do I find what jobs are best for me? After indicating preferences for 60 activities, answers are analyzed and users are told they "fit" into two of these six work groups: Realistic, Investigative, Artistic, Social, Enterprising, or Conventional. Each work group includes a list of related civilian and military jobs. The Personality Test links to the AdvisorTeam.com site where one can take the popular *Temperament Sorter II Instrument™* for measuring and understanding one's personality. Two separate reports (*The Classic Temperament Report™* and *The Career Temperament Report™*) are available for $14.95 and $19.95 each or $27.95 for both reports.

The Career Key   Assessment
www.careerkey.org/english

There is much more to this site than what initially appears to be an online self-assessment test. Operated by Lawrence K. Jones, Ph.D., Professor Emeritus in the College of Education at North Carolina State University, and his wife, Jeanine Wehr Jones, the site is well worth exploring for job search instruments, information, and advice. Using Dr. John Holland's _Self-Directed Search_, the site is designed to help users make better career decisions through self-assessment. Includes a free Career Key™ professional career test for measuring skills, abilities, values, interests, and personality related to particular jobs. After taking the online test, individuals are given scores on six personality types: Realistic, Investigative, Artistic, Social, Enterprising, and Conventional. They are then given a list of relevant jobs for each personality type. The online test takes about five minutes to complete. The site also includes many other useful career counseling tools and job search resources.

GSIA Carnegie Mellon   Assessment
http://web.gsia.cmu.edu/default.aspx?id=141459

Developed for students in the Graduate School of Industrial Administration (GSIA) at Carnegie Mellon University, this is a paper and pencil self-assessment exercise that generates a great deal of information on the individuals. It asks such questions as _"Describe yourself in one sentence," "What challenges you the most?," "How have you set yourself apart from the crowd?,"_ and _"What are the 10 most important things you are looking for in a job?"_ This site includes many other useful job search tools and information. It also includes a link to the CareerLeader™ program at Harvard University (www.careerdiscovery.com).

Jackson Vocational Interest Survey   Assessment
www.jvis.com

Enables visitors to take an online version of the Jackson Vocational Interest Survey, which takes about 40 minutes to complete. The

survey provides a detailed picture of an individual's career interests. It includes 289 pairs of job-related activities. The cost
($14.95) includes a detailed report showing your career interest
patterns with related matching occupations. The JVIS is especially
appropriate for high school and college students as well as for
adults interested in exploring new careers. The site also includes
several useful career resources relevant to education, career exploration, and other career websites.

Emotional Intelligence Quotient   Assessment
www.utne.com/interact/test_iq.html

Daniel Goleman's book, *Emotional Intelligence: Why It Can
Matter More Than IQ for Character, Health, and Lifelong
Achievement*, is the basis for this self-scoring instrument. Includes
10 multiple choice questions which yield a score that is translated
into your emotional quotient.

Emode   Assessment
www.emode.com/tests/career.jsp

This fun site includes several types of tests relating to personality,
romance, relationships, health, careers, and other aspects of life.
The career section includes 15 tests relating to everything from
personality, leadership, success, and risk-taking to IQ, power,
career makeover, career fit, and entrepreneurship. Even includes an
"Are You Millionaire Material?" and "The Coffee Test" tests.

Humanmetrics   Assessment
www.humanmetrics.com

This Israel-based company offers a free online version of the Jung-
Myers-Briggs typology for identifying your personality type. Also
offers a few other assessment devices, such as Small Business
Entrepreneur Profiler and Risk Attitudes Profiler.

Quick Personality Test   Assessment
http://users.rcn.com/zang.interport/personality.html

It doesn't get much quicker than this form and color test – just click onto the most appealing of nine shapes. The results sound very similar to your daily horoscope, which may actually yield better results!

Contacting a Career Professional

If you feel you need the testing and assessment services of a professional career counselor, especially someone you can meet with to administer and interpret test results, you should explore the many resources found on these five websites for career professionals:

- **National Board of Certified
  Counselors, Inc.**   www.nbcc.org

- **National Career
  Development Association**   www.ncda.org

- **Career Planning and Adult
  Development Network**   www.careernetwork.org

- **Career Masters Institute**   www.cminstitute.com

- **Professional Resume Writing
  and Research Association
  (PRWRA)**   www.prwra.com

For additional resources on career professionals who might be able to assist you with testing and assessment, please explore several websites identified in Chapter 12 on career counseling and coaching.

Microsoft eLearn

Microsoft

eLearn Home

LRN 3.0 Toolkit
LRN FAQs
eLearning Partners

Download the
LRN 3.0
Toolkit now...

Resources for Online
Learning...

Welcome to Microsoft eLearn

Here you will find the latest information about online content and resources available today from Microsoft and our eLearning vendors. By providing the enabling technology, content, and services in eLearning—our goal is to enable anytime, anywhere access to information for knowledge workers. Whether you are an educator, trainer, solution provider, global company, or just interested in what Microsoft is doing in the area of eLearning—we have something for you.

Enabling anytime, anywhere
access to information

University of Phoenix

CALL US AT
1·800·MY·SUCCESS

One University. Many Ways To Earn Your Degree.

▼ ONLINE PROGRAMS   ▼ FLEXNET® PROGRAMS   ▼ CAMPUS PROGRAMS

:University For Working Adults

At University of Phoenix, you can earn your bachelor's, master's or doctoral degree any way you want to—on campus, online, or in certain areas using a combination of both, which we call FlexNet®. University of Phoenix has grown to be the nation's largest private university, specializing in the education of working adults by offering degree programs that are highly relevant, accessible, and efficient. With over 100 campuses and learning centers in the United States, Puerto Rico, Canada and via the Internet, you can complete your degree no matter where you live, what hours you work, or how often you travel or relocate.

· Education for Corporations
· Become a Faculty Member
· Education for Military Personnel
· Student/Faculty Login

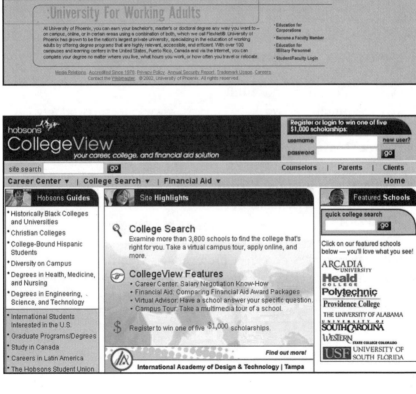

hobsons

CollegeView
your career, college, and financial aid solution

Register or login to win one of five $1,000 scholarships:

username   new user?
password   go

site search   go

Counselors | Parents | Clients

Career Center ▼ | College Search ▼ | Financial Aid ▼   Home

Hobsons Guides

* Historically Black Colleges and Universities
* Christian Colleges
* College-Bound Hispanic Students
* Diversity on Campus
* Degrees in Health, Medicine, and Nursing
* Degrees in Engineering, Science, and Technology
* International Students Interested in the U.S.
* Graduate Programs/Degrees
* Study in Canada
* Careers in Latin America
* The Hobsons Student Union

Site Highlights

🔑 **College Search**
Examine more than 3,800 schools to find the college that's right for you. Take a virtual campus tour, apply online, and more.

CollegeView Features
* Career Center: Salary Negotiation Know-How
* Financial Aid: Comparing Financial Aid Award Packages
* Virtual Advisor: Have a school answer your specific question.
* Campus Tour: Take a multimedia tour of a school.

$ Register to win one of five $1,000 scholarships.

Find out more!

International Academy of Design & Technology | Tampa

Featured Schools

quick college search
          go

Click on our featured schools below — you'll love what you see!

ARCADIA UNIVERSITY
Heald COLLEGE
Polytechnic
Providence College
THE UNIVERSITY OF ALABAMA
SOUTH CAROLINA
WESTERN STATE COLLEGE COLORADO
USF UNIVERSITY OF SOUTH FLORIDA

7

Education and Online Learning Sites

O NE OF THE BEST WAYS TO jump-start as well as advance your career is to acquire more marketable skills through formal education and training. Ongoing education and training are facts of life in today's workplace. Indeed, the skills you use today may become obsolete within the next few years. Staying marketable means constantly acquiring more education and training. While many employers operate in-house training programs, you are well advised to identify your own education and training needs in reference to your long-term career goals. Few people have valid excuses – other than avoidance – for not upgrading their skills given today's numerous educational and training opportunities. Many of these opportunities are low cost and available online.

Distance Learning

Distance learning has literally mushroomed over the past six years – from fewer than 500 distance learning programs in 1997 to over 6,500 institutions and more than 18,000 programs at the postsecondary level in 2003. It's a big and chaotic business chasing more than $120 billion in online educational dollars. The good news is that educational and training opportunities are widely available, in the classroom and online. The bad news is that potential students literally face an educational jungle out there – too many choices with too little information on the good, the bad, and the ugly.

If you lack marketable skills, wish to upgrade your skill level, or need to acquire new skills to change careers, you'll discover numerous websites available to assist you with all your education and training needs. Most of these educational institutions or training groups offer courses and degrees online. Almost every major university or college now offers some type of distance learning, distance education, continuing education, and/or Internet or online education. But one of the real innovators has been the once much criticized but now high-flying University of Phoenix (www.phoenix.edu), which enrolls over 90,000 students (the largest private university and often called by its jealous critics the "K-Mart of private business schools") and offers over 50 percent of its undergraduate and graduate degree and certification programs online, with students never having to set foot on a traditional college campus. Even traditional institutions, such as the University of Maryland University College (www. umuc.edu/gen/virtuniv.html) and Old Dominion University (www.odu. edu), have become pioneers in developing separate online undergraduate, graduate, and certificate programs. Many up and coming university programs, such as the highly targeted (military) American Public University System (www.apus.edu), offer 100 percent online bachelors, masters, and certification programs which are fully accredited.

Many of these education and training institutions and programs can be found by visiting the following gateway sites:

Peterson's	Education
www.petersons.com	

Peterson's, which is now part of the Thomson Learning empire, remains the leading publisher and distributor of information on educational programs. In fact, no one does it better than Peterson's, given its long history as well as recent merger with Thomson Learning, in compiling one of the most sophisticated and reliable educational databases. This site offers information on just about every type of education and training program available. It allows users to access a fabulous database on the following education and training programs and institutions:

- Colleges and Universities
- Graduate Programs
- Information Technology Programs
- Adult/Distance Learning Programs
- Training and Executive Education
- Private Schools
- Career Education and Guidance
- Summer Opportunities
- Study Abroad Programs

This site also is rich with information on college selection and includes online chats with education counselors. If you visit only one education and training site, make sure it's Peterson's.

CareerOneStop   **Education**
www.careeronestop.org

Previously part of the U.S. Department of Labor's separate website, America's Learning Exchange, this new employment resource site represents your tax dollars working for you. Its "Training and Education Center" section is well worth visiting for identifying education and training needs, locating education and training providers, and acquiring financial aid to achieve your education and training goals. This information also is included on its sister U.S. Department of Labor employment sites – America's Job Bank (www.ajb.gov), America's Career InfoNet (www.acinet.org), and America' Service Locator (www.servicelocator.org). Unraveling a great deal of America's education and training complex, from colleges and universities to government-sponsored training programs, the site includes linkages to numerous other sites, including several key associations, that have databases of education and training service providers. This site also includes linkages to websites that warn about scholarship and education scams, including the Better Business Bureau's site (www.bbbon line.org).

Distance Learning on the Net   Education
www.hoyle.com/distance.htm

Operated by distance learning guru Glenn Hoyle, this site functions as a directory to all types of distance learning programs,
products, and services on the Internet. The database includes adult
education and continuing education programs, training and
development programs for business and industry, colleges in North
America and abroad, conferences and events, courses and classes,
distance learning portals, K-12 education programs (including
home schools), associations and agencies, teaching resources,
technical and vocational programs, and vendors offering products
and services. A rich resource for locating education providers.

International Distance   Education
Learning Course Finder
www.dlcoursefinder.com

Education and training are truly borderless once you explore this
site. Claiming to be the world's largest online directory of e-
learning courses, this site includes over 55,000 distance learning
courses and programs offered by universities, colleges, and
companies in 130 countries. You can search the site by keyword or
course name, subject, country, or institution name. Also includes
a list of distance learning associations by regions.

MindEdge   Education
www.mindedge.com

This e-learning database and education infrastructure company
contains hundreds of education courses from over 30 educational
providers that offer online and classroom based courses. This site

allows users to browse 11 categories of distance learning programs and courses: teaching, business and management training, computers and IT training, engineering and math, law, social sciences, arts and humanities, health and science, degree programs, personal hobbies and self improvement, and foreign studies. The site also allows users to search by instruction type (CD, classroom, degree, online), category, and provider as well as enroll online for specific courses.

The Distance Education   **Education**
   and Training Council
www.detc.org

Formerly known as the National Home Study Council, this is the professional association and clearinghouse for the field of distance study/correspondence. Its more than 60 accredited members offer hundreds of courses in a variety of different distance learning formats and disciplines, from military training and truck driving courses to hospitality and hypnosis programs. Since many business schools and correspondence programs are controversial (often diploma mills operating on the edge with government educational assistance monies), you are well advised to visit this site for information on accreditation and members. Includes a directory of accredited institutions, subjects taught, degree programs, and useful resources.

Bear's Guides   **Education**
www.degree.net/books/bearsguide.htm

Two leading experts on distance learning, John and Mariah Bear (authors of _Bears' Guide to Earning Degrees by Distance Learning, College Degrees by Mail and Internet, Best MBAs by Distance Learning,_ and _Best Computer Degrees by Distance Learning_), offer advice on distance learning programs. The site also includes information on 100 of the top distance learning programs (click on to the "Schools" button at the top) and links to information on the distance learning arena (click on "Links").

Major Online Educational Programs

Leading educational institutions, publishers, and technology companies
have gone into the online education business within the past few years.
Five of the major players include the following:

University of Phoenix   **Education**
www.phoenix.edu

This is one of the real innovators in developing online education
and distance learning programs. It has surprised many traditional
universities, as it has become the largest university in the United
States, even though it has no central campus (it operates from
127 campuses and learning centers in 27 states, Puerto Rico, and
Vancouver, British Columbia). With over 90,000 students enrolled
in its many programs, the University of Phoenix grants traditional
undergraduate and graduate degrees as well as offers certificate and
special training programs. This site outlines its many programs and
services for students, faculty, corporations, and other parties.

Capella University   **Education**
www.capellauniversity.edu

Started in 1993, this innovative online university offers more than
600 courses relevant to undergraduate and graduate degree
programs in 40 areas of specialization. Currently offers degree
programs through the schools of business, education, human
services, psychology, and technology. Offers special programs for
military personnel, community colleges, and corporate employees.
Includes a quiz to find out if you fit the profile of a successful
online learner. A well organized site that will give you an up-close
look at what an online university is all about – from a virtual
library to alumni links.

Kaplan College   Education
www.kaplancollege.edu

This is a sleeper site – a lot more to what initially appears to be just another company offering online educational services. This is big and it's getting bigger. Kaplan College, which has been in the education business since 1937 and is now owned by the Washington Post Company, delivers educational programs via the Internet. As part of Kaplan, Inc. (www.kaplan.com), it's a leading provider of educational and career services, especially test prep and college admissions books and software. Offers several schools and programs of study: Business, Information Technology, Criminal Justice, Paralegal Studies, and Continuing Education. Markets extensively into the lucrative military, corporate, and international student ("no passport required") educational markets. One of the less expensive online educational programs, it currently costs $235 per credit hour to take courses through Kaplan College. Kaplan continues to be a major and growing player in the online education and career business, given the continuing integration of its various education and career businesses.

Education Direct   Education
www.educationdirect.com

Previously known as Harcourt Learning Direct, this company is now part of the huge Thomson Learning publishing empire. It has been providing distance learning services around the world for more than 100 years. It currently offers over 80 distance learning programs. The courses cover the fields of administration, building trades, computers, creative design, education, electrical/electronics, engineering, legal/medical, management, mechanical, security, and travel and hospitality. This company also offers a U.S. high school diploma and ASB (Associate in Specialized Business) and AST (Associate in Specialized Technology) degrees. The site also offers other online programs: California College for Health Sciences (www.cchs.edu), Business and Industrial Division for corporations, and over 3,000 business and industrial courses for Workforce Development programs (www.workforcedevelopment.com).

Microsoft eLearn   **Education**
http://microsoft.com/eLearn

Microsoft Corporation has entered the education field in a big way. In fact, this is Microsoft's online learning site which is linked to several "eLearning Partners." It offers numerous web-based training programs for individuals and companies. As might be expected, most of these programs focus on using Microsoft IT products.

A Wealth of Educational Sites

Numerous other websites offer an incredible number of online education and training opportunities as well as lots of information and advice about this often controversial arena. We recommend visiting the following sites for exploring various online courses, institutional options, and advice on making educational and training decisions. Several of the non-university companies offer a wide range of courses and certification programs aimed at individuals in need of improving their technical skills:

- **About Distance Learning**   www.distancelearn.about.com
- **Brainbench, Inc.**   www.brainbench.com
- **Continuing Education
  University 4 You**   www.ceu4u.com
- **Cyber U**   www.cyberu.com
- **Distance Education
  Clearinghouse**   www.uwex.edu/disted
- **Distance.Gradschools.com**   www.distance.gradschools.com
- **Distance Learning
  Resource Network**   www.dlrn.org
- **Electronic Campus**   www.electroniccampus.org
- **Entrinsik**   www.entrinsik.net
- **Globewide Network Academy**   www.gnacademy.org
- **Jacksonville University**   www.ju.edu

- Jones International University   www.jonesinternational.edu
- Mindleaders   www.mindleaders.com
- National Universities Degree Consortium   www.nudc.org
- National University Online   www.online.nu.edu
- OnlineLearning.net   www.onlinelearning.net
- Regis University   www.regis.edu
- Saint Leo University   www.saintleo.edu
- Search 4 Education   www.search4education.com
- SUNY Learning Network   www.SLN.suny.edu
- The University Alliance   www.universityalliance.com
- TeleClass.com   www.teleclass.com
- Thinq   www.thinq.com
- WorldWideLearn   www.worldwidelearn.com

Useful Associations and Companies

For more information on distance learning and online education and training, visit the following associations and companies:

- America's Distance Education Consortium   www.adec.edu
- Distance Education and Training Council   www.detc.org
- Distance Learning Channel   www.ed-x.com
- Distance Learning Resource Network   www.dlrn.org
- Educause   www.educause.edu
- International Association of Continuing Education and Training   www.iacet.org
- International Internet Learning Association   www.iila.net
- Learning Resources Network   www.lern.org
- United States Distance Learning Association   www.usdla.org

- University Continuing
  Education Association   www.ucea.edu
- World Association for
  Online Learning   www.waoe.org

Traditional Education Programs

Several websites focus on helping individuals locate colleges and universities which offer on-campus courses and programs. As noted above, Peterson's (www.petersons.com) includes a huge database on such educational institutions and programs. Two other websites also provide useful information on college selection and finance:

College Guide   Education
www.mycollegeguide.org

If you're looking for a traditional college or university campus for education and training, this site helps identify campuses that meet certain criteria, such as region, estimated annual cost, size of freshman class, surrounding community size, and school type. It also includes information about colleges and the two most important questions – how to get in and how to finance it all.

College View   Education
www.collegeview.com

If you're interesting in identifying the right college or university to meet your education needs, try the search features on this useful site. Users can search over 3,800 colleges by selecting 14 different criteria for finding the right "fit." The site also includes useful information on scholarships, test preparation, financial aid, and electronic applications, as well as includes a guidance office, career center, and bulletin board.

Career Explorer   **Education**
www.careerexplorer.net

This unique site is designed to help prospective students find
information on career opportunities and select the right schools for
pursuing educational and career goals. One of the few websites to
focus on exploring both education and career opportunities.
Includes both career and school search options, numerous links to
educational institutions, articles on selecting the best vocational
schools or colleges, financial aid tips, and career planning advice.

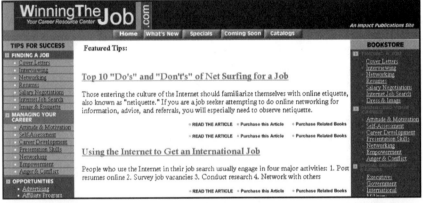

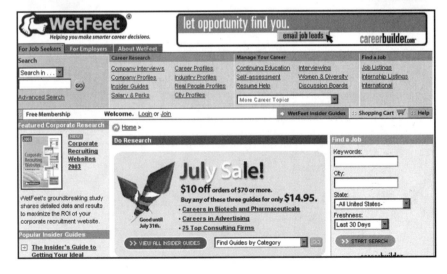

8

Career Information, Advice, and Research Sites

WHILE MOST EMPLOYMENT websites focus on the needs of employers with resume databases and job postings, some websites are primarily designed to assist job seekers with various steps in their job search. Often operated by career professionals rather than advertisers and entrepreneurs, these sites include a great deal of useful information, tips, and advice on how to conduct an effective job search: assessment, research, resumes and letters, networking, interviews, negotiations, and career services.

Career Information and Advice

You can find a wealth of career information on the Internet in the form of articles, quizzes, and directories dealing with everything from employment trends to salary negotiations. The following sites are especially noted for their collection of career information designed to assist job-seekers with various stages of the job search:

America's CareerInfoNet   Career Information
www.acinet.org

This is a really useful information-rich website designed to help job seekers, employers, human resource specialists, and workforce development specialists make smart career decisions based upon sound information about the job market. Once again brought to you by the government, ACINet is another U.S. Department of Labor career center linked to three other useful job centers – America's Job Bank (www.ajb.gov), America's CareerOneStop (www.careeronestop.org), and America's Service Locator (www.servicelocator.org). This site focuses on providing useful career information. It includes occupational outlook data from the latest edition of the *Occupational Outlook Handbook* as well as information on the fastest growing and declining occupations and those with the most openings, largest employment, and highest pay. Its "Career Tools" section includes a unique section called "Employability Checkup" where users can get some sense of how difficult it would be to find a similar job at a similar wage if they became immediately unemployed. This section also includes a useful employer locator, licensed occupations, job description writer, financial aid advisor, and a career exploration area which also includes several downloadable videos on a variety of occupations. The "Career Resources" section includes a library of more than 4,000 links to resources (articles and videos) that deal with hundreds of career issues, from employment and wage trends to researching employers, exploring job and resume banks, and acquiring relocation information. You'll also find useful information on wages, job requirements (knowledge, skills, and abilities), and state-by-state labor market information.

Riley Guide   Career Information
www.rileyguide.com

As noted in Chapter 4 on gateway employment sites, this site is the work of career librarian Margaret F. Dikel who clearly understands the job search process and has organized her massive database accordingly. It's presented around key categories that primarily relate to the needs of job seekers:

- What's New
- Prepare for a Job Search
- Resumes and Cover Letters
- Targeting and Researching Employers
- Executing Your Job Search Campaign
- Job Listings
- Networking, Interviewing, and Negotiating
- Salary Guides and Guidance
- Information For Recruiters
- A-Z Index

Each category includes annotated links to other sites that provide information, advice, or additional resources. For example, under Resumes and Cover Letters, the site includes a partial list of resume and cover letter books with links to the publishers as well as linkages to sites with information, advice, or services relating to CVs, portfolios, video portraits, and resume broadcasting. While never complete and with many gaps, nonetheless, this site compiles a wealth of job search information from other websites. The A-Z Index has it all!

Quintessential Careers **www.quintcareers.com**	**Career Information** **and Advice**

You can see the fingerprints of a career professional all over this site, which is primarily designed to help college students get into college and conduct an effective job search based upon a sound understanding of what ingredients should go into the job search. The job and career sections also are relevant to all types of job seekers – not just college students and recent graduates. As a major job and career portal, this site includes over 1,000 pages of content with numerous helpful career articles and linkages to other employment websites. Most of the articles are authored by Dr. Randall S. Hansen and Katharine Hansen who also are authors of the book *Dynamic Cover Letters* (see order form at the end of this book). The site also includes a "Career Doctor" Q&A section (with Dr. Randall S. Hansen and also found on www.careershop.com), a career tutorial section, and a free online newsletter. You'll want to bookmark this site and refer to it several times during your job search.

Vault.com	**Career Information**
www.vault.com	**and Advice**

This is a very busy site that takes some time to determine what it actually does, which is a lot of different things related to employment, job seekers, employers, and recruiters. You can easily get lost in its multiple channels and sections. Developed by the unsuccessful offline publishers of the *Vault Reports*, this flashy online venture capital operation is trying to be all things to everyone. In so doing, it offers a wealth of resources in the form of information, advice, and research. You can browse numerous message boards, ask career experts questions, have someone review your resume, network with others, read career news, sample one of Vault's career and industry guides (can purchase 19 different ones), and research selected companies. The site also has developed special communities dealing with law, finance, and consulting, as well as operates a bookstore. And, of course, the site includes a resume database and job postings. But it's an especially useful site for job seekers in search of information and advice on employers and various steps in the job search.

Wetfeet	**Career Advice**
www.wetfeet.com	**and Research**

This site specializes in providing a wealth of career information and advice to job seekers which it also syndicates to other employment websites. Consequently, you might find some of their articles on several websites we reviewed in Chapter 5. Wetfeet specializes in conducting employment research, producing short career news and job search articles. The "For Job Seekers" section of this site is divided to focus on the three actions job seekers need to take:

- Career Research
- Manage Your Career
- Find a Job

Its "Career Research" section is especially useful for job seekers interested in researching companies, careers and industries, locations, salary and perks, and publications. The "Manage Your Career" section includes numerous short articles on resumes, interviews, self assessment, and women as well as discussion boards. The "Find a Job" section includes job listings, internships, and international employment information.

Monster.com	Career Advice
http://content.monster.com	

This content section of the Monster.com mega site includes advice, tools, and tips on resumes, interviewing, salaries, networking, diversity, and relocation. It also offers specialized advice on various occupations, college to career, and work abroad. Offers a very rich collection of useful information for organizing an effective job search.

WinningTheJob	Career Advice
www.winningthejob.com	

This is our own career information, advice, and resource website. It's designed to provide job seekers and employees, from entry-level to CEO, with sound advice on finding jobs and managing their careers. Offering numerous tips for success in the form of one- to three-page articles, it includes expert advice on everything from developing a career objective, writing resumes and letters, networking, interviewing, and negotiating a compensation package for job seekers, to career development, empowerment, assessment, communication, stress management, and anger control for managing the day-to-day details of one's job. This site also is linked to our three other career websites that focus on career resources (books, videos, software) and syndicated career content:

- Career Bookstore   www.impactpublications.com
- Career Content   www.contentforcareers.com
- Military Transition   www.veteransworld.com

Several mainstream business magazines and newspapers offer excellent career articles and advice through their online sites. These four in particular are well worth bookmarking and visiting frequently:

- **Business Week**   www.businessweek.com
- **Fast Company**   www.fastcompany.com
- **Fortune**   www.fortune.com
- **Washington Post**   www.washingtonjobs.com

Several career experts, who have written books and/or write syndicated career columns for newspapers and magazines, also maintain their own sites or their content can be found on other sites that archive their numerous articles. In fact, you may find the tips and advice of these experts to be especially informative, since many are in a Q&A format and respond to current issues facing job seekers and employees:

- **Richard Nelson Bolles**   www.jobhuntersbible.com
- **Paul and Sarah Edwards** www.homeworks.com
- **Dale Dauten**   www.dauten.com
- **Anne Fisher (Ask Annie)** www.fortune.com/fortune/careers
- **Andrea Kay**   www.andreakay.com
- **Joyce Lain Kennedy**   www.sunfeatures.com
- **Carol Kleiman**   www.chicagotribune.com/classified/jobs/columnists
- **Ron and Caryl Krannich** www.winningthejob.com
- **Hal Lancaster**   www.careerjournal.com/columnists/careercorner
- **Fran Quittal**   www.careerbabe.com
- **Randall and Katharine Hansen** www.quintcareers.com
- **Rob Rosner**   www.workingwounded.com
- **Barbara Sher**   www.barbarasher.com

Career Research

Conducting an effective job search requires doing a great deal of research on jobs, companies, employers, and salaries. While much of this research function gets carried out during the process of networking for information, advice, and referrals, much of it should also take place on the Internet. Indeed, numerous websites offer rich databases for conducting research. These include company directories, listings of associations and nonprofit organizations, financial reports of publicly held companies (through SEC), company profiles, business news, and key contact information, including names, addresses, phone/fax numbers, and emails of officers.

If your research skills are a bit rusty, or if you're not sure where to start online, you should visit Debbie Flanagan's very useful website, which is actually a tutorial on how to research companies online for free. She takes you step-by-step through the research process, as well as provides hotlinks to all the major databases and research sites:

http://home.sprintmail.com/~debflanagan/index.html

Business Resources

CEO Express	Research
www.ceoexpress.com	

We really like this site for its wealth of in-your-face information. It doesn't get much more intuitive than a front page that lays out all its resource possibilities. This is the type of site you'll want to bookmark and refer to daily for information, from newspapers and magazines to news feeds and search engines. Pay particular attention to the "Business Research" section. This section unfolds with an incredible number of resources for conducting research on all aspects of companies. The small "Industry Center" button immediately to the right of the "Business Research" button and the "Company Research" subsection include numerous useful links to key resources. Be sure to spend some time exploring this gateway site. It's a remarkable research resource!

Dun and Bradstreet's   Research
Million Dollar Databases
www.dnbmdd.com/mddi

This is one of the most popular databases for researching nearly 1.6 million public and private companies in the U.S. and Canada with annual revenues in excess of $1 million. Its linkage to Dun and Bradstreet's International Business Locator provides access to over 28 million global companies in more than 200 countries. Includes a searchable database. Company information includes SIC code, size criteria (employees and annual sales), type of ownership, principal executives, and biographies. Covers everything from small to medium and large companies that voluntarily submit financial and contact data to Dun and Bradstreet (not all do). An excellent source for identifying and targeting companies, including names and phone numbers of key personnel. Individuals and companies must pay subscription fees to access this database and print out company reports. The site offers a sample report and free trial.

Hoovers   Research
www.hoovers.com

This popular site includes a wealth of information on thousands of companies in Hoover's database. It's especially useful for job seekers who wish to conduct research on particular companies as well as link to their websites and employment sections. While some of the information on this site is free, other more detailed research information is by monthly subscription fees only. Hoover's database includes company contact information, profiles, financials, and a link to the company's employment section. CareerBuilder.com has an advertising presence on this site and thus serves as Hoover's career center. A rich research and information site for understanding corporate America.

CorporateInformation   Research
www.corporateinformation.com

Operated by Winthrop Corporation, this is one of the best sites on the web for finding information on over 350,000 companies in more than 100 countries around the world. Over 20,000 companies are included in this site's database. Includes a variety of search engines for locating companies in the United States and abroad. Nothing fancy – just good search features that deliver the goods. Includes business news.

@brint.com, The BizTech Network   Research
www.brint.com

Wow! This is another excellent online resource for researching companies. It claims to be the premier business and technology portal and global community network for numerous fields of expertise as well as "Your survival network for the brave new world of business." Offering numerous channels, resources, and community networks along with three generations of business technology enterprises and reference sections, this is an incredibly rich site of business linkages. Includes numerous articles and the latest news on these cutting-edge fields. Users need to register in order to gain free access to this site. Includes numerous directory listings and a search engine. Enables users to translate the site into Spanish, German, French, Italian, and Portuguese.

AllBusiness   Research
www.allbusiness.com

This is one of the largest small business directories on the Internet with more than 700,000 companies in its database. It classifies businesses into nearly 9,000 categories. Includes numerous useful articles, forms, services, and checklists for eight major business categories: employment and HR; Internet and technology; office management; legal; sales and marketing; finance and accounting; business planning; and insurance. Offers a virtual gold mine of information for small businesses. In fact, it may motivate you to explore starting your own business rather than work for someone else! It's all here – sample business plans, legal advice, hiring/firing tips, financing, marketing, and lots more for developing a sound business.

BizWeb **www.bizweb.com**	**Research**

This business guide includes 46,290 companies listed in 208 categories. Just click on any business category and you'll get an alphabetical listing of companies with short 4 to 15 word annotations. Includes a keyword search engine.

Business.com **www.business.com**	**Research**

This high trafficked site (12 million visitors a month) offers one of the largest online directories for conducting business research. It's currently organized into over 25,000 categories and subcategories of businesses and includes more than 400,000 business websites. The site primarily offers detailed directory categories, a search engine, featured articles from such site partners as FastCompany and BusinessWeek, and sponsored links. A very rich site for conducting company research.

Thomas **www.thomasregional.com**	**Research**

One of the most reliable names in business directories offers free access to a searchable database of more than 550,000 distributors, manufacturers, and service companies in the United States. Users can browse over 6,000 product/services categories from a menu of over 100 main categories. Also covers, under "Business Resources," events and trade shows, government resources, and industry and professional organizations. Includes numerous useful resources for conducting online business research.

Other useful online databases and research tools for investigating companies, employers, and jobs include:

■ **Annual Reports**	www.annualreportservice.com
■ **Chambers of Commerce**	www.chamberofcommerce.com
■ **Daily Stocks**	www.dailystocks.com
■ **The Corporate Library**	www.thecorporatelibrary.com
■ **Harris InfoSource**	www.harrisinfo.com
■ **Inc. 500**	www.inc.com/500
■ **Moodys**	www.moodys.com
■ **NASDAQ**	www.nasdaq.com
■ **One Source Corp Tech**	www.onesource.com
■ **Standard & Poors**	www.standardandpoors.com
■ **Thomas Register**	www.thomasregister.com
■ **Wall Street Research Net**	www.wsrn.com

Several companies periodically publish lists which compare, rank, and rate the "largest," "top," or "best" companies, people, or places. *Forbes*, *Fortune*, and *Money* magazines include these lists on their websites:

www.forbes.com/lists

- ■ 100 Top Celebrities
- ■ 200 Best Small Companies
- ■ 400 Best Big Companies
- ■ 400 Richest Americans
- ■ 500 Largest Private Companies
- ■ 800 Best Paid CEOs
- ■ The Billionaires
- ■ Forbes 500s
- ■ Forbes International 500
- ■ Forbes/Milken Best Places for Business and Career
- ■ World's Richest People

www.fortune.com

- ■ 50 Most Powerful Women in Business
- ■ 100 Best Companies to Work For

- 100 Fastest-Growing Companies
- America's Forty Richest Under 40
- America's Most Admired Companies
- Best Companies for Minorities
- The Fortune e-50
- The Fortune 500
- The Global 500
- The Power 25: Top Lobbying Groups
- World's Most Admired Companies

http://money.cnn.com/best

- Best Places to Live
- Best Places to Retire

You may also want to regularly monitor several major business magazines which include a great deal of content on companies, executives, and employment trends as well as offer job search information and services. The following websites of business magazines and newspapers are well worth visiting:

Online Magazines

■ **Business Week**	www.businessweek.com
■ **Economist**	www.economist.com
■ **Fast Company**	www.fastcompany.com
■ **Forbes**	www.forbes.com
■ **Fortune**	www.fortune.com
■ **Smart Money**	www.smartmoney.com

Online Newspapers

■ **Investor's Business Daily**	www.investors.com
■ **Los Angeles Times**	www.latimes.com
■ **New York Times**	www.nytimes.com
■ **USA Today**	www.usatoday.com
■ **Wall Street Journal**	www.wsj.com
■ **Washington Post**	www.washingtonpost.com

Online Financial News

- Bloomberg   www.bloomberg.com
- CNNMoney   http://money.cnn.com
- Motley Fool   www.fool.com
- TheStreet.com   www.thestreet.com

These and many other online business publications can be quickly accessed through the front page of CEOExpress (www.CEOExpress.com).

Public Records Resources

EDGAR　　　　　　　　　　　　　　　　**Research**
www.sec.gov/edgar.shtml

This is the Filings and Forms (EDGAR) section of the U.S. Securities and Exchange Commission (SEC). The SEC requires that all public companies with assets in excess of $10 million and more than 500 shareholders must file registration statements, periodic reports, and other forms electronically through EDGAR. This information can be accessed and downloaded for free from this site. Just follow the Quick EDGAR Tutorial and you'll be able to research the records of thousands of public companies. You also can access the annual reports of numerous publically traded companies through a commercial website with a similar name: www.edgar-online.com.

Search Systems　　　　　　　　　　　　**Research**
www.searchsystems.net

This site includes 15,748 free searchable public record databases, organized by state and countries, and listed in alphabetical order. This is a surprisingly rich database for researching various aspects of communities, from corporations and libraries to properties and registered sex offenders in your neighborhood.

Association and Nonprofit Resources

| **Associations on the Net** | **Research** |
| **www.ipl.org/div/aon** | |

Part of the Internet Public Library, this is a gateway site to thousands of trade and professional associations, most of which are nonprofit organizations. If you are interested in working for an association or nonprofit or exploring opportunities with companies and organizations that belong to these associations (associations and nonprofits employ about 10 million people in the U.S.), this is a good site for locating such employers. The site primarily provides links to the associations. From there you can explore the associations. Many large associations maintain their own niche job banks and resume databases to service their member organizations. These are good sources for conducting research on member organizations and for exploring job postings. Many of the associations also maintain online links with their members and related groups and resources – a great source for exploring potential employers.

American Society of	**Research**
Association Executives	
www.asaenet.org	

The American Society of Association Executives (ASAE) is the professional association of association executives as well as the premier gateway site to over 6,500 associations. If you are interested in working for an association, you should belong to this professional organization. It has its own career center which includes a resume database, job postings, and several other job search services. Everything you ever wanted to know about careers in the association world can probably be found on this site. This also is a good site for researching who's who in the association world.

GuideStar   **Research**
www.guidestar.org

If you're interested in researching the world of nonprofit organizations, be sure to explore this rich site. It includes a searchable database of over 850,000 IRS-recognized nonprofit organizations. The site also includes numerous resources – from articles and reports – for better understanding the nonprofit sector. If you're interested in working in the nonprofit sector, this is site you'll want to visit and revisit in order to research the thousands of employers that make up this sector.

Action Without Borders   **Research**
www.idealist.org

Action Without Borders is the key gateway site to international nonprofit organizations, most of which operate in Third and Fourth World countries. Its searchable database includes 35,656 organizations operating in 165 countries. The site includes information on upcoming career fairs, a search engine to find services or programs in various countries, hundreds of useful nonprofit resources, and job postings for full-time, internship, and volunteer positions.

Several other websites provide useful information for researching the nonprofit sector, including job opportunities:

- **Charity Village (Canada)**   www.charityvillage.com
- **Council on Foundations**   www.cof.org
- **Foundation Center**   www.fdncenter.org
- **Independent Sector**   www.independentsector.org
- **Internet Nonprofit Center**   www.nonprofits.org
- **VolunteerMatch**   www.volunteermatch.org

Online Employment Resources

> **JobFactory**   **Research**
> **www.jobfactory.com**

Job seekers can access a great deal of information from this one-stop site. In addition to searching over millions of job openings by job title and geographical area by using the site's JobSpider search engine, JobFactory includes a list of 250 top career sites; links to classified job advertisements in 1,067 newspapers in the U.S., Canada, Asia, and Europe; a list of 3,787 job hotline telephone numbers (recorded vacancy messages); a database of 5,056 recruiters with online job postings; and links to 23,065 employer websites with job postings.

> **Job Search Engine**   **Research**
> **www.job-search-engine.com**

This site basically functions as a meta job search engine for locating job postings on the Internet. It searches eight top U.S. and Canadian job boards to identify job postings by keywords and location.

Declining Companies

While you can tell a lot about the financial health and growth prospects of companies by examining the above databases, at the same time you should beware of declining fortunes of many companies. As the high flying dot-com world of 2000 suddenly discovered, fortunes can quickly disappear in a volatile economy.

The following sites are worth visiting for tracking who's downsizing and possibly going out of business. These sites may raise some important questions that you should consider asking about the financial health and growth of a company before you accept a job offer:

- BankruptcyData   www.bankruptcydata.com
- Business 2.0   www.business2.com

     www.ecompanynow.com
- Dismal Scientist   www.economy.com/dismal
- Downside   www.downside.com
- Failure Magazine   www.failuremag.com

Career Masters Institute

Building Bridges Across The Careers Community

WELCOME TO THE CAREER MASTERS INSTITUTE™
Career & Employment Industry's First Global Training, Development & Professional Networking Organization

Membership & You

Professional Conference

Professional Credentials

Training Programs

Calendar of Events

Membership Directory
Bookstore
Contact Us
Board of Directors
Home Page

Members Enter

Our members come from every sector within the careers community - career coaches, counselors, outplacement consultants, resume writers, recruiters, college and university career development professionals, government and military career transition specialists, HR professionals and more. We've joined together to form the most vibrant careers association in the world.

Wendy S. Enelow, CPRW, JCTC, CCM
Founder & Executive Director

Impact Resume & Career Services

We write resumes that get interviews.

Home
Company Profile
Success Stories
Testimonials
Resume Samples
Services & Pricing
FAQ-How to Order
Career Resources
Contact Us

HOW MUCH ATTENTION WILL *YOUR* RESUME RECEIVE?
Only 15 to 30 seconds on first review!

A resume written by a **Certified Professional Resume Writer** is the key that opens the door to employment opportunities by clearly conveying your *qualifications, accomplishments* and *value.*

Don't prolong your job search with poorly written documents or ineffective search methods. *Our menu of services provides "one-stop shopping" for your job search success. All services are provided with the strictest confidentiality.*

☐ **Resume and cover letter composition** - MS Word, PDF and ASCII Text formats
☐ **Interview portfolio development** - Visually document your career progress
☐ **Interview preparation** - Prepare for Behavioral Based Interviews (BBIs)
☐ **Post-interview marketing letters** - A second chance to market your value
☐ **Customized job search planning** - Implementation of specific strategies to shorten your search time
☐ **Developing and improving your networking skills** - The #1 way to achieve your goals

---

e-resume.net™
Ranked *"best of the bunch"* -LA Times

July **29**

| HOME | ABOUT US | ORDER ONLINE | PRICES | OUR PROCESS | SAMPLES | CONTACT US |

WELCOME

e-resume.net is a national resume writing service company that combines personalized attention with the speed of the internet to deliver professional resumes.

TELL A FRIEND

If you are impressed with the convenience and service you've experienced here at e-resume.net, please tell your friends and associates. here

CAREER ADVICE

How is your **resume**?

don't **you wish** you were better prepared ▶

ORDER ONLINE

Ready... Set..Go!
Baffled about where to begin? Lost for words when it comes to "selling" yourself? Never enough time in the day to pull together your resume?
Let us do all the work!

Ⓐ **Get Your Resume Started Now!**
You can easily upload your current info and let us take care of the rest! (prices)

Ⓑ **Need More Info?**
Tell us your name, email and phone number and one of our Representatives will call you and answer your resume questions. (no charge)

Ⓒ Telephone us Toll Free:
1-866-277-5550

Ⓓ International customers (Outside USA & Canada)

9

Resume and Cover Letter Sites

R ESUMES ARE THE BREAD AND butter of the online employment business. Ironically, only a few years ago many career experts were predicting the end of resumes and the rise of portfolios and other forms of job search communication and applications. But the resume has become the perfect medium for online and scannable technologies as well as for email distribution systems. Without a dynamite electronic resume, your chances of being discovered in some faceless resume database are nearly zero. More so than ever, resumes are a necessary evil for imperfectly screening candidates.

Paper Resumes Becoming Nuisances

Given the high costs of managing paper resumes, more and more companies prefer receiving resumes by email or completing an online application form (candidate profile) in lieu of a resume. Indeed, for many companies it is now much easier and more cost effective to receive, scan, share, store, and retrieve an electronic resume or a profile than to handle a paper resume. As a result, some companies now discourage candidates from either mailing or faxing their resumes. Take, for example, Dow

Chemical. In 2001 it streamlined its hiring process with a new software system that only accepts electronic resumes. All resumes received in the mail are now automatically returned to the sender with a note saying that the prospective candidate must use the company's website to apply online with an electronic resume. In so doing, Dow Chemical reduced its average hiring time from 90 to 34 days and lowered the average cost of hiring by 26 percent as well as downsized its number of in-house recruiters from 100 to 60. Dow Chemical is not alone. As company websites become more sophisticated, and HR departments further automate the application and screening processes, paper resumes – whether scanned or hand processed – will no longer be the norm for communicating qualifications to employers. They are becoming obsolete. The trend is very clear, at least for large companies that must handle thousands of applicants and their resumes each year – HR departments increasingly prefer electronic emailed resumes or candidate profiles that are compatible with their hiring databases.

Resumes and Cover Letters

There's something mystical or magical about resumes. While they are job seekers' calling cards for getting job interviews, when placed online they seem to take on a different life. Job seekers enter them into a mysterious resume database and wait to be called for interviews. Somehow their electronic resume is expected to work its way up into the offices of hiring officials.

The same holds true for cover letters. Many career professionals note that a well crafted cover letter is often more important to landing a job interview than a resume. How both resumes and letters best get distributed is often the key to understanding effectiveness. In the meantime, the mystery goes on!

Resumes Play a Renewed Role

How technology has changed the role of resumes and given these documents renewed importance in the employment process! Indeed, the business model defining the structure of most major employment websites focuses on the key role of the electronic resume – sites are designed to attract job seekers' resumes into searchable databases as well as quickly transmit resumes to employers. The resume, whether in electronic or paper form, is the medium by which job seekers initially connect with employers. The important questions center around resume content and how to best distribute one's resume – whether passive or active – to potential employers.

The Hunt for Resumes

The larger the resume database, the more attractive a site becomes to employers who pay higher fees to search the larger databases. Sites must constantly recruit job seekers to their operations (just "Post Your Resume") and persuade them to enter their resume into the site's resume database – an all-seasons' "hunt for resumes." Sustaining, as well as increasing, the number of resumes in the database is by no means an easy task, nor is it cheap to do so. Resumes quickly become dated and thus must be updated or replaced by resumes of new job seekers.

As a job seeker, you are constantly being hunted by online employment sites.

As a job seeker, you are constantly being hunted by online employment sites that offer free resume services in the form of entering your resume into their online database and managing it through several of the following options:

- create and store multiple versions of the resume
- revise the resume(s) whenever necessary
- maintain privacy or anonymity through coding options and separate email accounts
- incorporate a job search agent that automatically emails you when a new job listing matches your criteria

You write the resume and upload it into their database, or you enter information about yourself into a standardized online resume form. These sites want your resume because they, in turn, have paying customers – employers and recruiters – looking for resumes from which to select candidates for job interviews.

The New Resume Entrepreneurs

At the same time, you're also being hunted online by professional resume writers and entrepreneurial email distributors who charge you for their specialized resume services. Many of them have linkages on a site's career resource or links section, present themselves in banner or button ads, or maintain affiliate or partnership relationships with the site on a shared revenue basis. Their pitch is always the same – the quality of your writing and distribution can be greatly enhanced by buying into their resume services. Indeed, when it comes to dealing with resumes, there is always room for improvement!

Numerous entrepreneurs are in the online resume writing and distribution business. This is a big business, from offering professional resume writing services to persuading individuals of the efficacy of "shotgunning" or "blasting" their resume to thousands of employers and recruiters. For the most part, these are not certified career counselors nor trained career professionals; most are professional writers who primarily write and produce resumes for a living. Some belong to organizations that issue professional credentials in this area.

From writing to distribution, this is both a mysterious and lucrative business. In fact, being mysterious probably contributes to making this such a good business. Services of a professional resume writer, for example, usually cost anywhere from $100 to $600, depending on the level of your position – executive-level resumes are the most expensive to produce. Signing up for the services of a resume distributor, who will blast your resume to a special list of employers and recruiters who supposedly want to see your resume, usually costs from $19.95 to $199.95.

Resume and Letter Writing Tips

Many employment websites will include tips on how to write winning resumes and letters. These often come in the form of short one- to two-page articles that list the "do's" and "don'ts" of both traditional and electronic resumes. Several sites maintain an inventory of such tips in the "Career Resources" or "Resource Center" section:

- Monster.com   http://resume.monster.com
- America's CareerInfoNet   www.acinet.org/acinet

- JobStar   www.jobstar.org/tools/resume
- CareerBuilder   www.careerbuilder.com
- Quintessential Careers   www.quintcareers.com
- Wetfeet   www.wetfeet.com
- JobWeb   www.jobweb.com
- WinningTheJob   www.winningthejob.com

A few sites, such as www.vault.com, even provide a free online resume review by a career professional. Other sites, such as www.careerbuilder.com ("Advice & Resources") and www.flipdog.com ("Resource Center"), primarily include sponsored links to companies that offer fee-based resume writing and distribution services. Resume writing professionals, such as author Rebecca Smith, maintain their own websites (www.eresumes.com) with tips on writing an electronic resume.

Professional Resume Writers

You'll have no problem finding individuals who will help you write both conventional and electronic resumes. Many can be found through your local Yellow Pages. Others maintain websites which showcase resume writing tips, testimonials from satisfied clients, and examples of their work. Indeed, the Internet is a huge shopping mall for identifying professional resume writers.

Our experience with resume writing is confirmed by many other career professionals. While most individuals can benefit from reviewing resume writing principles and examples of outstanding resumes, when it comes time to actually write their resume, they fall short in producing a first-class document. Writing a one- to two-page resume is hard work and requires special talents. Contacting a professional resume writer, with the experience and skills to produce a resume that reflects your talents, may well be worth $100 to $600, especially if it produces expected results – attracts the right employers to you. If and when you feel you need to contact a professional resume writer, you should consider exploring the resume writing talent associated with the following associations that certify resume writers and other career professionals:

- National Resume
  Writers' Association   www.nrwa.com

- Professional Association
  of Resume Writers and
  Career Coaches   www.parw.com

- Professional Resume
  Writing and Research
  Association   www.prwra.com

- Career Masters Institute   www.cminstitute.com

For an online state-by-state directory of professional resume writers –
which also includes a useful comparative chart for surveying service fees,
years of experience, certification, samples, and free critiques – visit the
NetWorker Career Services' (NCS) site:

http://careercatalyst.com/resume.htm

At the same time, check out some of these websites which are sponsored
by professional resume writers. Most of them will give you a free resume
critique prior to using their fee-based services:

- **A&A Resume**   www.aandaresume.com
- **A-Advanced Resume Service**   www.topsecretresumes.com
- **Advanced Career Systems**   www.resumesystems.com
- **Advanced Resumes**   www.advancedresumes.com
- **Advantage Resume**   www.advantageresume.com
- **Best Fit Resumes**   www.bestfitresumes.com
- **Cambridge Resume Service**   www.cambridgeresume.com
- **CareerConnection**   www.careerconnection
- **Career Resumes**   www.career-resumes.com
- **CertifiedResumeWriters**   www.certifiedresumewriters.com
- **eResume (Rebecca Smith's)**   www.eresumes.com
- **e-resume.net**   www.e-resume.net
- **Executiveagent.com**   www.executiveagent.com
- **Free-Resume-Tips**   www.free-resume-tips.com
- **Impact Resumes**   www.impactresumes.com
- **Leading Edge Resumes**   www.leadingedgeresumes.com
- **Resume Agent**   www.resumeagent.com
- **Resume.com**   www.resume.com

- **ResumeMaker**   www.resumemaker.com
- **Resume Writer**   www.resumewriter.com
- **WSACORP.com**   www.wsacorp.com

This is only a small sampling of the hundreds of professional resume writing services available to assist you with all your resume writing, and sometimes distribution, needs. We highly recommend using a professional at critical points in your job search, which may be here!

Resume Distribution Services

Resume distribution approaches have always been controversial, whether offline or online. Indeed, career counselors usually caution job seekers about literally "throwing money to the wind" by shotgunning, or blasting, their resumes to hundreds of employers. This is usually the approach of unfocused, and often desperate and unrealistic, job seekers. The experience is usually the same: few if any worthwhile returns. Like direct-mail responses, one can expect less than a one percent return rate. If you mail your resume to 10,000 potential employers, chances are you'll get fewer than 100 responses and even fewer than 10 positive responses. There's also a good chance you'll get zero responses for all the time, effort, and costs involved in this unfocused "wishful thinking" approach to finding a job.

The old adage that you usually get what you pay for is equally valid for the job search. . . . To be effective with this approach, you need to be the perfect ($$$) candidate.

Such an approach and response rate may convince you that *"No one wants to hire me!"* and you may further lose your self-esteem or get depressed in the process.

There's no reason to think that this direct-mail approach to the job search gets any better when you shift mediums – from snail mail to electronic mail – by blasting your resume to hundreds of employers and recruiters by email. Nonetheless, numerous resume distribution companies would make you believe this is an effective way to market your resume. They operate resume blasting businesses that usually charge anywhere from $19.95 to $199.95 to email your resume to hundreds of employers and recruiters; a few charge thousands of dollars for more specialized blasting service. Many of them post testimonials from satisfied clients who claim great success using this approach. But as any direct-mail specialist will tell you, response rates are largely determined by the quality of both the mailing list and the mailing piece. When the two come together, expect a good response rate. The problem is that you never know the quality of the email lists of these companies until *after* you use them.

We still remain skeptical about using this approach to marketing your resume. In fact, we have yet to meet any employers who would subscribe to such a questionable service. Few reputable recruiters actually use such services. While blasting your resume by email may make you initially feel good – because you are doing something and have high hopes of reaching many potential employers and recruiters – motion does not equate momentum. In the end, it may be a waste of time and money, accompanied by dashed expectations. Indeed, if you want to quickly experience the highs and lows of conducting a job search, this approach will surely provide such an experience. Resume blasting largely violates a key principle of conducting an effective job search that leads to an excellent job "fit" – target specific employers around your specific career goals, skills, and experience. Shooting a resume en mass to hundreds of employers and recruiters is not a very targeted approach. It's a "pot luck," and sometime desperate, approach to finding any job you think you might be able to fit into. We strongly recommend that you find a job that is fit for you. You do this with a more targeted approach.

Having said all of this as a cautionary note for taming your expectations, you may still want to blast your resume for under $50, just to see if you get any "nibbles" on this type of fishing expedition. If you are executive-level material, who wants to get your resume in the hands of many recruiters in your industry, you might get "lucky" with this approach. If you are an experienced professional, go ahead and spend $19.95 with www.resumeblaster.com to blast you resume to thousands of recruiters in your industry. At that price you don't have much to lose and perhaps you'll actually make a few useful contacts with recruiters. But again, don't believe all the hype surrounding this approach and have realistic expectations of what you are likely to get for only $19.95, or even $199.95. The old adage that you usually get what you pay for is equally valid for the job search.

Chances are your greatest success with this approach will come in having reached key recruiters or headhunters rather than specific employers – individuals who are primarily interested in marketing candidates who are skilled and experienced enough to make over $60,000, but preferably over $100,000, a year. These individuals are in constant need of new resumes to refresh their pool of fast-aging resumes and candidates who find jobs. Indeed, some recruiters and headhunters welcome the receipt of such blasted resumes which they, in turn, can "flip" to employers for hefty finders fees, if and when one of the candidates gets a job through their "recruiting" efforts. Their sourcing "commission" is usually 20 to 30 percent of the candidate's first-year salary, which is paid by the employer. In other words, you need to be the perfect candidate for this approach. If, for example, you are making under $50,000 a year, this approach is probably a waste of time and money. Most recruiters simply don't have time, nor a market, for such low-end candidates. This approach is one way to quickly reach hundreds of recruiters whom you might not reach by other means, such as putting your resume online with www.brilliantpeople.com or www.recruitersonline .com. Indeed, if you are a near or over six-figure job seeker, you can quickly rachet up your job search, as well as go global, by using these services to contact thousands of headhunters or executive recruiters who are always looking for high quality resumes and candidates they can market to their high-paying clients. The approach does work, but it works best for only certain types of candidates who fit the needs of recruiters and headhunters.

If and when you decide to play this game – knowing full well the odds are probably against you – start by investigating the following fee-based resume distribution firms (your cyberspace "blasters"). Try to find out the relative mix in their database of recruiters versus actual employers who might be looking for someone with your qualifications. These sites know the "mix" since they require employers and recruiters to sign up or register to receive "free" resumes from these services. For example, one of the largest such firms, www.resumezapper.com, tells you up front that they only work with third party recruiters and search firms – no employers; they primarily appeal to candidates who prefer being marketed through an executive recruiter. The recipients of these free resumes usually specify filters, so they only receive resumes that meet their marketing criteria. Not surprisingly, most of these resume distribution sites will blast your resume to almost solely to recruiters or headhunters. Some sites, such as www.resumeagent.com and www.resumerabbit.com, will blast your resume to numerous sites that have resume databases, thus saving time in entering your resume into each unique resume database.

- **BlastMyResume**   www.blastmyresume.com
- **Careerxpress.com**   www.careerxpress.com
- **DeliveryMyResume**   www.deliverymyresume.com
- **E-cv.com**   www.e-cv.com
- **Executiveagent.com**   www.executiveagent.com
- **HotResumes**   www.hotresumes.com
- **Job Search Page**   www.jobsearchpage.com
                             (international focus)
- **Job Village**   www.jobvillage.com
- **Nrecruiter.com**   www.nrecruiter.com
- **Resume Agent**   www.resumeagent.com
- **ResumeBlaster**   www.resumeblaster.com
- **Resume Booster**   www.resumebooster.com
- **ResumeBroadcaster**   www.resumebroadcaster.com
- **Resume Path**   www.resumepath.com
- **Resume Rabbit**   www.resumerabbit.com
- **ResumeSubmit**   www.careerxpress.com
- **ResumeZapper**   www.resumezapper.com
- **ResumeXpress**   www.resumexpress.com
- **RocketResume**   www.rocketresume.com
- **See Me Resumes**   www.seemeresumes.com
- **WSACORP.com**   www.wsacorp.com

Do It Right

As many job seekers discover when incorporating the Internet in their job search, their resume plays a key role in the whole Internet job search process. Above all, employment sites, employers, and recruiters want your online resume. Therefore, make sure you produce and distribute a first-class resume that truly reflects your skills and accomplishments. As we've outlined in this chapter, you'll find numerous online resources to help you at every stage of developing and distributing your resume. Our advice: Make sure you also visit the many assessment and testing sites identified in Chapter 6, as well as perhaps visit a professional career counselor (Chapter 12), to help you focus your resume, and your job search, around what you do well and enjoy doing. If you do this, you'll find a job that best fits you rather than try to fit into a job description that may or may not be appropriate for you. The Internet is a great tool for connecting with employers. Just make sure you're making a **quality connection** with a top quality resume that reflect the "real you."

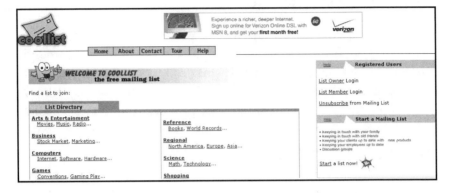

coollist

| Home | About | Contact | Tour | Help |

WELCOME TO COOLLIST
the free mailing list

Find a list to join:

List Directory

Arts & Entertainment
Movies, Music, Radio...

Business
Stock Market, Marketing...

Computers
Internet, Software, Hardware...

Games
Conventions, Gaming Play...

Reference
Books, World Records...

Regional
North America, Europe, Asia...

Science
Math, Technology...

Shopping

help **Registered Users**

List Owner Login

List Member Login

Unsubscribe from Mailing List

help **Start a Mailing List**

· Keeping in touch with your family
· Keeping in touch with old friends
· Keeping your clients up to date with new products
· Keeping your employees up to date
· Discussion groups

Start a list now!

10

Networking, Mentoring, and Q&A Sites

I F YOU'RE LOOKING FOR QUALITY JOBS and wish to shorten your job search time, be sure to initiate an ongoing networking and mentoring campaign designed to acquire employment information, advice, and referrals. You'll find numerous networking and mentoring opportunities both online and offline. Many of the Usenet newsgroups listed in Chapter 3, for example, function as important networking arenas for asking and responding to questions and for acquiring useful information, advice, and referrals. At the same time, numerous websites also serve as important centers for performing these same functions.

Networking Sources, Skills, and Strategies

As many career professionals emphasize, networking plays a critical role in the whole job search process, from beginning to end. While the most effective networking takes place in face-to-face situations, you also can do a great deal of e-networking on the Internet. As noted in Chapter 3, be sure to check out these Usenet newsgroups for online networking opportunities:

- Google   www.groups.google.com
- Topica   www.topica.com
- Yahoo!   http://groups.yahoo.com
- MSN   http://groups.msn.com
- Newzbot   www.newzbot.com
- Usenet Info Center   www.ibiblio.org/usenet-i/
                        home.html

Also, visit these four sites for finding, or creating, mailing lists related to your career interests:

- Coollist   coollist.com
- Google   groups.google.com
- Topica   topica.com
- Yahoo! Groups   groups.yahoo.com

Many of the mega employment groups outlined in Chapter 5, such as Monster.com, have very active chat groups and message boards through which you can network for information, advice, and referrals. Indeed, the Monster.com boards are among the best on the web:

http://networking.monster.com/messageboards

If you're uncertain how to network, or if your networking skills are somewhat rusty, you are well advised to visit these websites for information and advice on how to sharpen your networking skills:

- WetFeet   www.wetfeet.com/advice/
                         networking.asp
- Monster.com   http://networking.monster.com
- Quintessential Careers www.quintcareers.com/
                         networking.html
- Riley Guide   www.rileyguide.com/netintv.
                         html
- WinningTheJob   www.winningthejob.com
- SchmoozeMonger   www.schmoozemonger.com
- Susan RoAne   www.susanroane.com/free.html
- Contacts Count   www.contactscount.com/
                         articles.html

While there are no good online substitutes for a well developed book on networking (see, for example, *Masters of Networking, Foot in the Door, How to Work a Room, Great Connections, The Power to Get In, Power Schmoozing, Power Networking, Smart Networking,* and *The Savvy Networker* – see order form at the end of this book or browse online through www.impactpublications.com), these sites will get you started in the right direction.

Associations As Networks

One of the best networking sources is through membership and activities in professional and trade associations. Many professional associations, such as the American Society for Training and Development (www.astd. org) and the Society for Human Resources Management (www.shrm.org), have numerous active local chapters that provide excellent networking opportunities. They also operate niche online career centers – complete with resume databases, job postings, and career resources – for their members. To find a professional association most closely related to your professional interests, be sure to explore these gateway sites to the world of trade and professional associations as well as related nonprofit organizations:

- **Associations on the Net**   www.ipl.org/ref/AON
- **AssociationCentral**   www.associationcentral.com
- **American Society of Association Executives**   www.asaenet.org
- **GuideStar**   www.guidestar.org

Women's Networks

Several organizations are specifically set up to encourage networking among their members. Women, in particular, may belong to several organizations that encourage networking, from business and professional groups to alumni and social groups. Some of the major women's online networking groups include:

- Advancing Women www.advancingwomen.com
- American Association of
  University Women www.aauw.org
- American Business
  Women's Association www.abwahq.org
- Business Women's
  Network Interactive www.BWNi.com
- Federally Employed Women www.few.org
- iVillage www.ivillage.com
- Systers www.systers.org
- Women.com www.women.com

In the Washington, DC area, women professionally involved with web development and design ("new media") have created one of the best networking organizations available anywhere – complete with discussion groups and job postings:

www.dcwebwomen.org

If you are female and travel a lot, you'll appreciate this very unique networking site for women who want to make connections in unfamiliar places – the ultimate web-based long distance networking tool:

www.HERmail.net

This site could also be used for establishing long distance networking contacts for purposes other than just travel.

Alumni Groups for Networking

If you are a college graduate, one of the best places to network is through your college alumni office. Many universities operate alumni networks ostensibly designed to raise financial support from alumni but which also offer excellent opportunities for graduates to make face-to-face contacts with fellow graduates for employment information, advice, and referrals. Alumni are often asked if they would be willing to speak with other alumni about career-related matters. If they agree, they are flagged in the alumni database as someone who would be willing to help fellow graduates network. Please check with your college career center or alumni office for such formalized networking opportunities. If, for example, you are a business school graduate from one of the "elite" institutions, you may be associated with one of higher education's best organized alumni network groups. According to a *Business Week* study in 1996, the business schools at the following institutions had the strongest and weakest alumni links (www.businessweek.com/1996/43/b349812.htm):

School	MBA Alumni (Percent Giving)	Average Gift	MBA Alumni Clubs
Strong Links			
▪ Dartmouth	6,818 (63%)	$418	17
▪ Virginia	5,655 (47%)	610	18
▪ MIT	5,500 (37%)	350	16
▪ Stanford	22,172 (31%)	684	47
▪ Duke	6,521 (31%)	418	14
▪ Harvard	35,378 (30%)	1,860	110
Weak Links			
▪ Berkeley	26,455 (10%)	$496	15
▪ Indiana	11,000 (11%)	134	3
▪ Thunderbird	28,442 (13%)	123	81
▪ Texas	9,350 (14%)	136	0
▪ Rochester	7,243 (15%)	100	1

Most of these universities, as well as many of their schools and departments, have dozens of local alumni chapters throughout North America and abroad where members occasionally meet to raise funds for programs, assist graduates, and develop and strengthen personal and professional contacts with one another. As recent studies have noted, it's often the quality of the networking experience at universities – rather than the content of the educational curriculum – that is the key determinant of career success. Harvard and Stanford universities, for example, are noted for the important role networking plays in the careers of their successful graduates. These institutions first and foremost recruit smart people into their programs and then provide a unique networking environment where students work together and form lasting bonds that often play a critical role in their continuing career success even 10, 20, or 30 years after graduation. Magazines, such as *BusinessWeek Online* (www.businessweek. com), offer unique opportunities for business school students to network online. You also should explore a few alumni sites which provide access to thousands of alumni networks around the world:

- **Alumni.net**   www.alumni.net
- **Alumniconnections**   www.bcharrispub.com/isd/
                             advanced_directory.html

Locators for Re-Building Networks

What ever happened to your old friend John Nebor whom you last saw in Minneapolis three years ago at your tenth high school reunion? Remember your favorite college professor whom you worked with on a special marketing project in 1995 but whom you heard moved to another university in 1999? No problem; they may be just a quick click away.

You can use the Internet to find old friends and acquaintances you may have lost contact with over the years but whom you want to contact for networking purposes. Include these sites in your "network finder" folder:

- **Anywho**   www.anywho.com
- **Classmates**   www.classmates.com
- **InfoSpace**   www.infospace.com
- **KnowX**   www.knowx.com
- **Reunion** (high school)   www.reunion.com
- **Switchboard**   www.switchboard.com
- **The Ultimate White Pages**   www.theultimates.com/white
- **Whowhere Lycos**   www.whowhere.lycos.com
- **WorldPages**   www.worldpages.com
- **Yahoo**   www.people.yahoo.com

Military Locators and Buddy Finders

If you are in the military or if you are a veteran, you can check the location of your service buddies by going to these people finder sites, which include personnel locators and missing buddies bulletin boards:

- GI Search.com   www.gisearch.com
- Military.com   www.military.com
- Military Connections   www.militaryconnections.com
- Military USA   www.militaryusa.com

Job Search Clubs and Support Groups

Other networks involve displaced workers and over-40 job seekers who literally form job search networks, job clubs, or support groups for the purpose of conducting a job search based upon networking principles. Most of these groups are organized at the local level, especially in major metropolitan areas, and offer free or inexpensive job search assistance. Check these sites to see if there is such a group functioning in or near your community:

- 5 O'Clock Clubs   www.fiveoclockclub.com
- 40-Plus Clubs   www.40plus.org/chapters
- Chicago Jobs   www.chicagojobs.org/network. html

- ExecuNet   www.execunet.com
- Professionals in Transition   www.jobsearching.org

You also may find job search networks, clubs, and support groups associated with colleges and universities, women's centers, churches, YMCA's, and local social service organizations.

Mentors, Career Coaches, and Q&A

Online career advice comes in many different forms, from short one- and two-page how-to articles, to chat groups, bulletin boards, "Ask the Expert," "Job Doctor," and "Q&A" sections. Unfortunately, much of what goes on in relatively unstructured and amateur-driven chat rooms is noise that can be distracting, misleading, and frustrating to job seekers who readily admit that they must be "doing something wrong," because they are not getting expected results from their job search efforts. Such forms of advice are usually found within a "Job Resources" or "Career Center" section.

Our advice: Skip most of the amateur noise and accompanying

anarchy – which is usually brought to you by people who don't have a clue what they really should be doing – and visit an experienced expert who knows what he or she is talking about. Some of the most valuable online career advice comes from experts or career professionals who serve as a combination career coach and mentor. Recognizing that the job search is by nature a lonely, difficult, and at times ego-deflating experience – often filled with many rejections and dashed expectations – mentors extend a helping online hand as they assist job seekers in dealing with various aspects of the job search, especially the many bumps and bruises along the way. As coaches, they help provide structure to the process and reassure job seekers that this process does indeed work for those who are well organized, purposeful, talented, persistent, and enthusiastic. Numerous well established fee-based career management firms, such as Bernard Haldane Associates (www.jobhunting.com), R. L. Stevens and Associates (www.interviewing.com), and Right Management Consultants (www.right.com), serve as professional career coaches who lead job seekers through a very well defined and structured process, from career assessment to salary negotiations (see features on these firms in Chapter 12). Like a personal career coach, these experts provide job seekers with a structure as they help them stay focused on what's really important by using smart strategies and techniques that work.

When it comes to getting good career advice, be sure to visit some of the major sites we've already recommended:

- **Monster.com**   www.monster.com
- **Quintessential Careers**   www.quintcareers.com
- **Vault.com**   www.vault.com
- **WetFeet**   www.wetfeet.com

Numerous other mentoring resources are available on the Internet. The following two are directories to these resources:

- **Peer Resources**   www.peer.ca/mentor.html
- **Find a Mentor**   www.findamentor.org

The **Women's Executive Network** (www.wxnetwork.com) attempts to link girls ages 16-19 with female executives who serve as role models.

Once on the job, a few sites offer mentoring services to deal with the day-to-day realities of work:

- **Career Systems International** www.careersystemsintl.com
- **Deliver the Promise** www.deliverthepromise.com

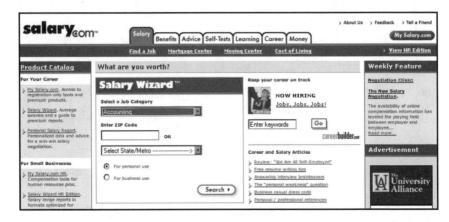

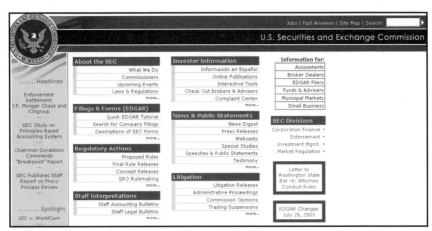

11

Interview, Salary, and Relocation Sites

WHILE MOST EMPLOYMENT websites focus on connecting job seekers with employers through the use of resumes and job postings, a few other sites include useful information on the critical job interview, salary negotiation, and relocation steps of the job search. In fact, after experiencing the euphoria of being invited to a job interview, many job seekers quickly discover a new reality – the job interview is the most critical step in the whole job search process – no interview, no job offer, no job. If you handle the job interview well, you'll most likely receive a job offer as well as negotiate salary and benefits commensurate with your level of skills, abilities, and accomplishments.

Interviews Count the Most

Your resume may get you an invitation to the job interview, but it's your interview skills that will determine whether or not you will get the job. And it's usually during the final interview that you negotiate a compensation package that will influence the direction of your future compensation. Neglect these critical steps in your job search and you will be back to chasing down more employers with your resume to invite you to more job interviews.

If you review the many websites identified in this chapter, you should be able to better prepare for the job interview and salary negotiation steps. While none of these sites substitute for a good book on interviewing and salary negotiations (see the order form at the end of this book for recommended titles), they at least introduce you to many issues involved in this critical stage of your job search. You'll be a wiser, and hopefully more capable, job seeker for having visited these sites.

Interview Preparation and Practice

Many major employment websites, such as Monster, CareerBuilder, HotJobs, FlipDog, Vault, WetFeet, and CareerJournal, include information on job interviews. This is usually found in the resource center, career advice, or job tips section and comes in the form of one- to two-page articles on interview mistakes, sample questions, and interview preparation. Some sites may include a self-scoring interview quiz, a career coach dispensing interview advice, or an interactive practice interview which enables job seekers to select alternative answers (multiple choice) to a variety of questions often asked by interviewers. Most of the interview information and advice is free, although a few sites, such as WSACorp. com, charge for the services of an online career coach who assists individuals in preparing for the job interview. Such insights, advice, and practice sessions can help prepare you for the critical job interview. However, these online services should supplement, rather than substitute for, one-on-one interview preparation. While the Internet is a wonderful tool for initially screening candidates and employers, only a fool would hire an unknown over the Internet. In the end, the most critical step in the job search – the job interview, which could end up being several interviews with the same employer – is conducted in face-to-face situations where employers and recruiters have a chance to assess both your verbal and nonverbal interpersonal skills. In

> *While the Internet is a wonderful tool for initially screening candidates and employers, only a fool would hire an unknown over the Internet.*

such encounters, where first impressions mean a lot, the final outcome may be determined as much or more by your dress, handshake, eye contact, speech patterns, timing, and listening skills than by the content of your messages. In other words, the job interview is more about determining your likability and social competence than your technical qualifications. These are critical "job qualification" elements that cannot be determined through online communication.

Useful Job Interview Sites

In preparation for the job interview, we recommend visiting these websites which are primarily devoted to preparing job seekers for the critical job interview:

Monster.com   **Job Interviews**
http://interview.monster.com
http://content.monster.com/jobinfo/interview

As might be expected, Monster.com includes excellent sections on interview preparation. The first section offers practice interviews ("Virtual Interview") for a variety of occupational fields, including feedback on one's performance and tips on thank-you letters, second interviews, and negotiations. The second section includes tips on virtual interviews, questions to ask interviewers, using the telephone, and responding to tough questions. Taken together, these two sections offer some of the most useful interview preparation tips on the Internet.

InterviewPro   **Job Interviews**
www.interviewpro.com

This free site includes a database of over 1,600 interview questions which are organized around various occupations. Also includes sample competency-based interview questions. Registered users can submit new categories of questions, ask questions, and access questions not available to non-registered visitors.

JobInterview.net   Job Interviews
www.job-interview.net

This is a rich site for exploring numerous aspects of the job interview for both job seekers and employers. Includes numerous practice questions, mock job interviews, 900+ sample questions for 41 job functions, expert interview advice, a seven-step interview plan, and a downloadable ($19.95) interview preparation book. Interview advice for job seekers is provided by career authors Matt and Nan DeLuca (*Best Answers to the 201 Most Frequently Asked Interview Questions* and *More Best Answers to the 201 Most Frequently Asked Interview Questions*). In fact, much of what you will find in their interview books can be accessed for free through this site. The site also includes a job interview resource section.

Interview Coach   Job Interviews
www.interviewcoach.com

Operated by "Interview Coach" Carole Martin, this site is designed to assist job seekers in preparing for the job interview. Includes practice interview questions to test your interview skills. Offers an "Interview Fitness Training" workbook (print and downloadable versions) and fee-based telephone and in-person coaching services. For those who need one-on-one interview coaching services.

Other good online sources for interview tips include these two gateway sites, which are loaded with a combination of articles and linkages to other interview and compensation sites:

- **Quintessential Careers**   www.quintcareers.com/intvres.html
- **Riley Guide**   www.riley.com/netintv.html

Also, check out several university career center sites fro job interview tips. The MBNA Career Services Center at the University of Delaware, for example, includes a useful online career guide with sample interview questions and dressing advice:

www.udel.edu/CSC/guide.html#Article15

Look for other university career centers through the Career Development/Catapult section of NACE's JobWeb.com site (see page 66 for details).

Salary Negotiation and Compensation Sites

Salary negotiations are one of the most important yet most neglected job search steps. In the end, it's your talent in exchange for salary, benefits, and perks. How well you negotiate your compensation package may well determine your long-term financial worth to this and other employers. However, few people are savvy salary negotiators. They often don't know what they are really worth in today's job market and are hesitant to talk about money. As a result, many job seekers accept the first salary offer, which may be 10 to 20 percent lower than what they could have gotten had they followed some very basic salary negotiation techniques.

Several books, including our own _Dynamite Salary Negotiations_ and _Get a Raise in 7 Days_, outline how to best negotiate a compensation package to your advantage. At the same time, a few websites include tips from these books as well as important salary data for determining salary comparables. If you want to know what you are worth in today's job market, wish to better understand various elements in compensation packages, and need to hone your salary negotiation skills (what to say and when to say it), be sure to check out several useful websites that focus on this critical salary negotiation step in the job search. Some of the best salary negotiation sites to visit in preparation for addressing compensation issues include:

Salary.com	Salary Negotiations
www.salary.com	

This site has quickly become the premier salary site, and for good reasons. It includes a wealth of useful information for dealing with compensation issues. Its "Salary Wizard" provides quick access to salary comparables in numerous metropolitan areas and for hundreds of job categories and position descriptions – a good place to start researching what you are potentially worth in particular geographic areas. Many other employment websites incorporate Salary.com's Salary Wizard into their site for addressing questions concerning salary comparables. The site also includes salary news, salary advice, discussions, and career resources. Job seekers also can search for jobs through this site.

JobStar.org   Salary Negotiations
www.jobstar.org

This site is operated by a library system in northern California. It includes one of the most useful linkage sections on salary surveys, which currently includes over 300 general and professional salary surveys found on the web (from "Accounting" to "Warehousing"). Also includes a "Salary I.Q." assessment test, tips on negotiating salaries, and linkages to salary articles. You also may want to explore other useful sections on this site related to resumes and career guides.

Monster.com   Salary Negotiations
http://content.monster.com/salarylinks
http://content.salary.monster.com
http://forums.monster.com/forum.asp?forum=107

These three sections within the mega Monster.com employment site include several useful linkages to salary-related websites, numerous articles on key compensation issues and negotiations strategies, and salary calculators and tools. It also includes an interesting "Salary and Negotiation Tips" message board that includes numerous questions and answers from novice job seekers and Monster.com's "The Salary Negotiation Expert."

Wageweb   Salary Negotiations
www.wageweb.com

Primarily designed for employers, this HR salary service site includes compensation information on over 170 benchmark positions. Includes salary data on several categories of positions, such as Human Resources, Finance, Engineering, Healthcare, and

Manufacturing. Organizations and consultants can join Wageweb for $169 and $219 per year respectively. Individuals can review some salary data as well as several job descriptions. The site also includes frequently asked questions and links to HR websites.

Robert Half International   **Salary Negotiations**
www.rhii.com

Robert Half International claims to be the world's first and largest specialized staffing service. Focusing on staffing temporary, full-time, and project professionals in the fields of accounting and finance, administrative support, information technology, law, advertising, marketing, and web design, Robert Half International has 320 offices in North America, Europe, Australia, and New Zealand. The company is especially well known for its annual salary guides that cover the positions for which they provide staffing services. You can request a complimentary copy of their Salary Guide as well as three other career-related guides through this site's "Resource Center" or the "Career Center" section of it's related OfficeTeam (www.officeteam.com) site. Just complete the request form indicating which guides you wish to receive. The site also includes useful resources on resumes, cover letters, interviewing, and links to other sites. Individuals can browse job openings and submit resumes online.

Abbott-Langer   **Salary Negotiations**
www.abbott-langer.com

Another site primarily designed for HR professionals and compensation specialists in need of highly specialized, and somewhat pricey, compensation data. Abbott, Langer, and Associates, Inc. publishes salary survey information on over 450 benchmark jobs in information technology, marketing/sales, accounting, engineering, human resources, consulting, manufacturing, nonprofit, legal, and other fields drawn from data on more than 7,000 participating organizations. While the site offers free summary data for several positions, reports cost from $100 to $795 each. The site also

includes information on its HR and management services as well
as a collection of useful HR articles.

**Securities and Exchange   Salary Negotiations
   Commission
www.sec.gov**

The U.S. Securities and Exchange Commission maintains compensation data on high-level executives through its EDGAR database.
If you plan to earn in excess of $500,000 annually, you should
visit this site for compensation information on companies registered with the SEC – those with more than 500 investors and $10
million in assets. Also see page 120.

**SalarySource.com   Salary Negotiations
www.salarysource.com**

This site is rich with salary information and tips, including a
database for assessing the market value of 350 benchmark
positions by city. However, very little is free on this site. It costs
$19.95 per inquiry to access the salary data. The site does include
informative articles on compensation and lots of job descriptions.

Other compensation-related sites worth visiting for addressing various
aspects of the job negotiation process include:

- BenefitsLink   www.benefitslink.com
- BenefitNews.com   www.benefitnews.com
- Bureau of Labor Statistics   www.bls.gov
- CareerJournal   www.careerjournal.com
- CompGeo Online   www.claytonwallis.com/cxgonl.
                               html

- Employee Benefit
  Research Institute   www.ebri.org
- PayScale   www.payscale.com
- Quintessential Careers   www.quintcareers.com/salary_
                               negotiation.html

- Realtor.com   www.homefair.com

- Riley Guide   www.rileyguide.com/netintv.
                                   html
- SalaryExpert   www.salaryexpert.com
- SalaryMaster   www.salarymaster.com
- Salary Surveys for
  Northwest Employers   www.salarysurveys.milliman.com

Relocation Sites

Much of life is a transition – moving from one location to another. Indeed, a large percentage of jobs require relocation. If you want to quickly advance your career – or change your life – you should seriously consider moving to a community that offers greater career and lifestyle opportunities. Changing your environment can have a major, and positive, impact on your career and life.

So, pull out a map and start dreaming about where in the world you would like to live and work. What are the comparative advantages and cost differentials of working in various communities, or even countries if you plan to become an expatriate? What do you know about the quality of schools and health care, the cost of housing, recreation and entertainment opportunities, and various community services and lifestyle opportunities available in other communities? When it comes time to consider relocation options, especially calculating the cost of relocating into a compensation package, you are well advised to visit several websites that address a multitude of questions relating to relocation issues – from calculating cost of living differentials to contacting a mover to take all your "stuff" to another location. Many of the sites outlined in this chapter include salary calculators useful to job seekers who need to know the differences in the cost of living between communities. These calculators basically indicate how much your salary in Community X is worth when compared to the cost of living in Community Y – information you need to know before accepting a job offer in a different community. After all, a $200,000 house in your present community may cost $350,000 in another community, which may effectively wipe out any salary gains you may think you are making by changing jobs. Each of these websites can provide useful information for making salary, relocation, and lifestyle decisions.

The following sites provide a wealth of information on relocating to thousands of communities in the United States and abroad. Use these sites for researching communities, locating housing, calculating the local cost of living, checking out schools and restaurants, investigating local cultural opportunities, and identifying community organizations and services.

Realtor.com   Relocation
www.homefair.com

This is one of the Internet's premier relocation sites which also powers the relocation section of many employment-related websites. Includes a wealth of information on dozens of important issues and questions affecting relocation decisions – cities, schools, crime, lifestyle, insurance, finance, employment, cost of living differences, planning, home ownership, professional movers, packing tips, storage, taxes, and moving to a new state. Includes a useful "moving through this life transition" section that includes sections on graduating, getting a job, getting married, raising children, getting promoted, emptying the nest, and retiring. If you've ever been reticent about pulling up stakes, this site will surely help in easing the transition.

MonsterMoving   Relocation
www.monstermoving.com
www.virtualrelocation.com

Operated as part of Monster.com, this site addresses numerous issues relating to both domestic and international relocation. Includes sections on finding a home, shopping for a mortgage rate, finding a mover, changing addresses, planning and managing a move, and living and shopping in a new community. The international section includes information on everything from visas to selecting an international moving company.

Relocation Central   **Relocation**
www.relocationcentral.com

There's a lot more to this site than what initially appears on a rather simple front page. The site includes relocation service information organized by state/city and category. If, for example, you select a specific city, you'll find a tremendous amount of information on the community to help you plan your move – from banks to weather. A good site for exploring numerous aspects of various communities both before and after making a relocation decision. Also includes numerous tools and tips, relocation checklists, a human resources directory, international relocation linkages, school comparison reports, roommate services, an apartment directory, and much more.

Runzheimer International   **Relocation**
www.runzheimer.com

Runzheimer is one of the oldest, largest, and most trusted names in the international relocation and travel business. Designed primarily for government agencies and corporations, this site includes information on Runzheimer's many domestic and international relocation services. Also includes a revealing two-location cost of living comparison service (fee-based).

Job Relocation   **Relocation**
www.jobrelocation.com

Designed for executive-level candidates and recruiters facing critical relocation decisions that make the difference between accepting and rejecting a job offer, this site includes several useful free services and tools: cost-of-living reports, home-selling assistance, relocation package, cost-of-living counseling, and personalized recruiter and job candidate consultations. Includes a few useful articles and links. Operated by salesman-realtor-web designer-relocation specialist Steve Levine.

| **Homescape** | **Relocation** |
| www.homescape.com | |

This site primarily focuses on housing (finding and financing) and the moving process. Includes sections on buying a home in 25,000 cities, applying for a loan, searching for an apartment, selling a home, and locating a moving company or truck rental firm.

For other useful relocation information, including tips from the U.S. Postal Service, a complete book on relocation (*Insiders' Guide to Relocation*), and international relocation services, visit these sites:

- 123Relocation.com   www.relo-usa.com
- Employee Relocation Council www.erc.org
- GMAC Relocation Services   www.gmac-relocation.com
- Going Global   www.goinglobal.com
- Insiders' Guide   www.insiders.com/relocation
- MoversNet   www.usps.gov/moversnet
- Moving.com   www.moving.com
- MovingCost.com   www.movingcost.com
- Relocate-America   www.relocate-america.com
- Relocation-net.com   www.relocation-net.com
- Wall Street Journal   www.homes.wsj.com

12

Career Counseling and Coaching Sites

S OME JOB SEEKERS ARE self-starters who can pick up a job search book, follow each step in the job search process, and land their dream job within a few weeks. Bless them – they are true entrepreneurs who are focused on what works and they become successful despite encountering numerous rejections on the potholed road to job search success. However, the truth is that very few people are that entrepreneurial or successful on their own – perhaps five percent. However self-assured, positive, and talented they may be, most job seekers need some professional help.

But selecting and using a career professional can also lead to disappointments. The career business is populated by a very diverse mix of professionals and wannabees. Certification is often lacking or very lax. Some self-declared career professionals are known for engaging in fraud or taking advantage of vulnerable clients who are in desperate need of finding a job. If and when you decide to seek professional career assistance, you should do so based upon the information found in this chapter for identifying such services. For in the end, it should be your money in exchange for the very best career assistance talent you can buy.

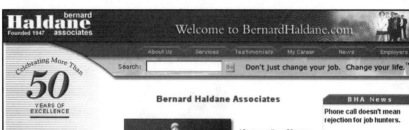

Haldane
bernard associates
Founded 1947

Welcome to BernardHaldane.com

About Us | Services | Testimonials | My Career | News | Employers

Search: [ ] [Go] **Don't just change your job. Change your life.™**

Celebrating More Than **50** YEARS OF EXCELLENCE

Newsletter
Get the latest career news and insight from Bernard Haldane Associates sent free, right to your e-mail.

Subscribe today!

[Enter E-mail]

○ **Yes!** Send me career

Bernard Haldane Associates

After more than 50 years of experience helping clients re-evaluate, reshape and rejuvenate their careers, we discovered that there are a number of critical "career situations" that job seekers may face at various stages in their careers.

WHAT IS YOUR SITUATION?

BHA News
Phone call doesn't mean rejection for job hunters.

Many job hunters misinterpret receiving a phone call, as opposed to a letter, as a lack of interest. Instead, these "screening calls" frequently mean that the resume has sparked an employer's curiosity. The company simply wants more information before committing to a face-to-face interview.

More News | Video News

DBM

JULY 29, 2003

SEARCH | GO!

Bookstore | Contact Us | Press Room | Site Map

▶ ABOUT DBM
▶ HR CHALLENGES
▶ CAREER SOLUTIONS
▶ NEWS & RESEARCH
▶ DBM WORLDWIDE

○ Please Select a Country.

Join DBM's Online Community of HR Professionals

WHAT'S NEW
Watch a video showing how this DBM client went from 0 to 140 networking interviews in just weeks

TOOLS AND TIPS
Find out why you should provide senior executives with specialized solutions.

HR REALITIES
Help your college graduate child bridge the gap between graduation and his or her first paycheck.

CERTIFIED CAREER COACHES

Welcome to
CertifiedCareerCoaches.com
The first and only exclusive website of listed certified career coaches serving clients worldwide!

▶ Home Page
▶ Find My Coach
▶ Become Listed
▶ Member Log In
▶ Resume Posting
▶ Press Releases
▶ Contact Us

NETWORK

Career Masters Institute

CertifiedCareerCoaches.com connects you with credentialed career coaches who provide expert advice, guidance, and support to those who seek career success! Career coaches take a personal interest in the success of their clients and will take the time to learn about you and what you want to gain from your next career move.

If you answer YES to any question, a career coach can help!

* Do you want a different career, but not sure what?
* Do you want to build a valuable network, but don't know how?
* Are job opportunities being missed because of your interview skills?
* Do you fear career success because of what others might expect of you?
* Do you want more control of your job situation or conducting your job search?
* Is it difficult for you when it comes to negotiating your salary?
* Is transitioning from a military career to civilian your next career step?

Click here to locate your personal certified coach who can meet your specific career coaching needs. Our career coaches provide coaching services by phone or in person. Please let them know you found them by using our website.

All career coaching credentials and organizational memberships have been verified by CertifiedCareerCoaches.com. Each listed career coach is ...

* certified by a supporting professional career coaching organization

Self-Starters and Wishful Thinkers

Despite wishful thinking, most job seekers are not self-starters who can run with a self-directed book or put together a successful self-directed job search campaign based on tips from other people, including websites. Indeed, most job seekers get high on expectations but low on implementation. They may understand what they need to do in order to make the process work for them, but in reality they don't do it right. Their very first step should be self-assessment – discover what they do well and enjoy doing – but instead they start by writing their resume and then blast it to hundreds of potential employers and recruiters. Preoccupied with the trees rather than seeing the whole forest from start to finish, they never get back to basics by doing a proper self-assessment. Instead of making 25 new contacts this week (five per day), they only make two new contacts as part of their networking campaign, retreat to their computer to "surf the web" for jobs, and then complain about how difficult it is to find a job. They eventually land a job, but it's often not the right one, because they never really put together a well organized and implemented job search campaign focused around their major strengths. As in the past, they become "accidental job seekers" who fall into jobs. They will most likely repeat this process in another year or two, once they discover they fell into a job that was not really a good fit for their particular interests, skills, and abilities.

> *Most job seekers get high on expectations but low on implementation. However self-assured, they need help.*

Regardless of what other people might say about doing the job search on your own, most job seekers can benefit tremendously from the assistance of a career counselor, career coach, or other type of career professional who can provide you with a structure for organizing and implementing a well-targeted job search campaign. As you will quickly discover, a successful job search is all about structure and implementation. And that's where a career professional can play a critical role in helping you through what is often a difficult process – more difficult than you might ever imagine. Whatever you do, don't dismiss professional help in your job search. As many job seekers before you have discovered, a career professional may be your very best friend throughout this process.

A professional may cost you some money, but he or she also may give you a tremendous return on your investment, which may be immediately reflected in your new salary which you negotiated with the assistance of your career professional.

A Season for Everything

There's a season for everything. In the case of the job search, you may quickly discover that it's the season to seek professional help for organizing and implementing a successful job search. After all, your next career decision will probably have important implications for your future income and lifestyle. Do it right, and you may be forever enriched with a job that is both financially and personally rewarding. Do it wrong, and you may soon be looking for another job which you hope will be better the next time. Look at it this way: the next job you accept will probably be worth $250,000 to $1 million, depending how long you stay. Is this the type of investment you want to make haphazardly on your own, or could you benefit from the expertise of a career professional who might be able to guide you into the right direction that could possibly double the worth of your next job?

Career Management Firms

Many executive-level candidates often use the services of professional career management firms which charge clients for career coaching services. These fees can run from $2,000 to $5,000, depending on the company and the services required. Most of these firms include one-on-one self-assessment, resume writing, and career coaching services. They work with clients, helping them develop effective marketing, networking, interviewing, and salary negotiation skills to ensure they are successful in finding a job; these are not employment or placement firms that find clients jobs. While many career counselors and job seekers may criticize these firms because they charge substantial fees for services that are available free through public sources (schools, community colleges, and community career centers), on the other hand, most of the free services are not geared toward executive-level candidates. Better still, many job seekers who use these fee-based career management services are thrilled with the outcome – they landed the perfect job that also paid far more than they could have received had they bootstrapped this process on their own. For example, they paid $4,000 for the career management services and ended up with a terrific job that paid $20,000 more than their last job. Conclusion: It was indeed a wise investment to contract with a professional career management firm to help guide them through this difficult process. They likely would not have achieved the same outcome on their own or through the many free career counseling services available through public sources.

Four of the most respected fee-based career management firms work with a variety of clients, from companies experiencing downsizing to individuals making $50,000+ a year. They include the following:

Bernard Haldane Associates   Career Management
www.jobhunting.com
www.bernardhaldane.com

This company represents the retail side of career management with its focus on individual job seekers who pay for a suite of job search services. Representing the oldest (50+ years) and one of the largest career management firms (600,000+ clients), Bernard Haldane Associates has pioneered much of today's leading career management, coaching, and counseling methods. Indeed, its founder, Dr. Bernard Haldane, is literally the father of modern career counseling. Beginning in the 1940s, his methods have been incorporated in most job search books (the basis for the popular *What Color Is Your Parachute?*) and career counseling practices. Such concepts as the information or referral interview, Success Factor Analysis, and "T" letters come from this source. Bernard Haldane Associates currently operates over 90 offices in the United States, Canada, United Kingdom, Australia, and the UAE. Clients work closely with a Career Advisor who coaches them through the job search process, from assessment to salary negotiations. Individuals can continue using these services at no additional charge for three years after finding a job through the Haldane organization. The job search methods used by this firm are outlined in five books published by Impact Publications (see order form at the end of this book): *Haldane's Best Resumes for Professionals, Haldane's Best Cover Letters for Professionals, Haldane's Best Answers to Tough Interview Questions, Haldane's Best Salary Tips for Professionals,* and *Haldane's Best Employment Websites for Professionals*. These books constitute one of the most thoroughgoing libraries for organizing and implementing an effective job search, including the use of the Internet. Haldane clients have access to the company's proprietary online job search service, CS2K (Career System 2000), which consists of a huge database of online job search tools for researching companies, jobs, and key individuals. Many of the firms that compete with Bernard Haldane Associates use similar methods, because many of their owners were once associated with the Haldane organization. The other firms, however, tend to focus on providing outplacement services to corporate clients who sponsor career management services for their departing employees. Only a few Haldane offices include corporate outplacement in their menu of services.

Right Management Consultants   Career Management
www.right.com

This international career management and human resources firm operates more than 200 offices worldwide. It provides career services to numerous corporate clients, especially those dealing with downsizing and requiring outplacement assistance. Most job seekers who work with Right Management Consultants receive free career management services because they are paid for by a sponsoring organization, which is most likely their employer who has just fired or "separated" them from the company. Right Management Consultants also provide customized online career management and outplacement services for their corporate clients through their proprietary website – online consulting, research tools, self-assessments, targeted job banks, and networking opportunities. This company also maintains an online database of resumes to market their clients' ex-employees.

Drake Beam Morin   Career Management
www.dbm.com

Drake Beam Morin (DBM) has been a leader in the fields of outplacement consulting and career transition services. It provides, for example, career transition services to the U.S. Olympic Team. Operating 230 offices in 51 countries, including China, Russia, and Australia, DBM primarily works with organizations that are downsizing their workforces and require the career management services of a firm such as DBM. They also work with HR professionals to enhance their hiring and retention programs. This site includes lots of informative sections on DBM's services, articles, tips, and resources. The fastest way to navigate this site is to go directly to the site navigation button on the left. Since Drake Beam Morin is in the process of being sold (was recently part of the Thomson publishing empire), the structure of this website is likely to change with the owners.

> ## R. L. Stevens & Associates   Career Management
> ## www.interviewing.com

This firm offers fee-based career management services to individuals who wish to change jobs or careers, as well as corporate outplacement services. The site outlines the company's approach, includes a map of its 16 U.S. offices, presents job search articles, and offers proprietary services to its clients.

Other firms offering similar or related career management and outplacement services include:

- CareerLab   www.careerlab.com
- Career Management
  International   www.cmi-imi.com
- Five O'Clock Club   www.fiveoclockclub.com
- Lee Hecht Harrison   www.lhh.com/us
- The Transition Team   www.transition-team.com
- WorkLife Solutions   www.worklife.com

Certified Career Counselors

Where can you quickly find a career counselor, especially one who has been trained and certified? Trained and certified career counselors have usually completed a two-year graduate training program in counseling from a recognized university. The following two websites focus on certified career counselors

---

National Board of Certified   **Career Counselors**
    Counselors, Inc.
www.nbcc.org

This organization certifies counselors in several areas: career counseling, school counseling, clinical mental health counseling, and addiction counseling. Maintains a register of certified counselors.

National Career   **Career Counselors**
    Development Association
www.ncda.org

The National Career Development Association (NCDA) is a division of the American Counseling Association. Its stated purpose is to promote everyone's career development. Made up of career professionals, NCDA sponsors professional development activities, publishes, conducts research, and promotes professional standards. It trains and certifies Career Development Facilitators. Includes a useful section entitled "Consumers and Job Seekers."

Commercial Career Coaching

Several other organizations are involved in certifying a variety of career professionals who are not necessarily career counselors. These range from career coaches to professional resume writers. Certification of these individuals may involve everything from taking a short $200 "training" course to completing a series of professional development courses. Most members of the following organizations have a passion for promoting career development.

Career Masters Institute   **Career Coaching**
www.cminstitute.com

This organization focuses on certifying career specialists (CCM – Credentialed Career Master) as well as providing a professional network for exchanging information and advice relevant to its members, who consist of many freelancers and small business owners. Includes online training programs, conference information, and tools for improving professional competence and business development. A complete listing of CMI members, by profession and specialization, can be found by searching the "Online Member Directory" or in the Appendix of the president's (Wendy S. Enelow) two books, *Best Resumes for $100,000+ Jobs* and *Best Cover Letters for $100,000+ Jobs* (see order form at the end of this book). Users can search for a member by the following professional categories:

- Authors
- Business School
- Career Coaching
- Career Counseling
- College/University Placement
- Corporate - General
- Direct Mail Service
- Human Resources
- Internet Service and Sites
- Job Lead Report
- Military/Government Transition
- Outplacement
- Publishing
- Recruitment
- Reference Checking Service
- Resume Writing
- Secretarial Service
- Software and Information Technology
- Stationery Products
- Training and Development

Certified Career Coaches   Career Coaches
certifiedcareercoaches.com

This site pulls together a large number of career professionals who have been certified by a variety of organizations:

JCTC   Job and Career Transition Coach (certified by The Career Planning and Adult Development Network)

CCM   Credentialed Career Master (certified by the Career Masters Institute)

CEIP   Certified Employment Interview Professional (certified by the Professional Association of Resume Writers and Career Coaches)

The site functions as a gateway to these professional career certification organizations. A handy search engine lets users of this site find a certified career coach by city, state, country, company, specialty, and type of consultation. Career specialties include:

- Career Assessment
- Career Training and Development
- Career Transition
- International Interview Coaching/Salary Negotiation
- Interview Coaching/Salary Negotiation
- Job Performance Enhancement
- Military to Civilian Employment

Professional Association of   Career Coaches
Resumes Writers and Career Coaches
www.parw.com

This organization certifies individuals who want to become a Certified Employment Interview Professional (CEIP). Many members also are Certified Professional Resume Writers (CPRW).

The site includes search engines to find members by name, city, country, state, province, or area code. Its members are listed by name, address, phone number, email, and home page. Most members are either freelance career specialists or operate small resume-writing businesses. If you need a professional resume writer to help you with your resume, this is a good place to start shopping for such career expertise.

Association of Career Professionals International **Career Coaches**
www.acpinternational.org

This is the professional association of career management professionals. Consisting of a network of hundreds of career experts, it draws most members from the United States (914), Canada (214), United Kingdom (146), and Australia (50). You can search for an expert by country, state, and area of expertise. Areas of expertise include:

- Assessment
- Career Centers
- Career Management Educators
- Career Management Media
- Coaching
- Employee Retention
- Executive Recruitment
- Family/Spouse Relocation
- Financial Planning
- Internal Career Development
- Organizational Development
- Outplacement
- Personal Development
- Retirement Planning

Career Planning and Adult Development Network
www.careernetwork.org
Career Coaches

Operated by career development specialist Richard Knowdell, this website consists of a network of career professionals whose membership entitles them to a newsletter, journal, and access to other services, including certification workshops for job and career transition coaches and a very popular annual conference of career development professionals. The centerpiece for this site is its annual international career development conference which normally draws over 1,000 career professionals. Also certifies Job and Career Transition Coaches (JCTC) and Job Search Trainers.

13

Employer and Recruiter Sites

S INCE MANY EMPLOYMENT websites are designed for employers and recruiters, it's not surprising to find numerous sites
sponsored by these online players. Indeed, the economics of
online recruitment are such that both employers and recruiters
have much to gain by using the Internet to screen candidates for job
interviews. They basically want to scan through lots of resumes in order
to locate the perfect candidates.

Executive Recruiters and Candidates

The Internet is a double-edged sword for headhunters or executive
recruiters. On the one hand, the Internet is the executive recruiter's best
friend, because it is an efficient place to find resumes from which to
screen candidates for corporate customers. On the other hand, the
Internet can be the recruiter's worst nightmare, because many employers
are getting smart about online recruitment: they can bypass expensive
recruiters and go directly to online recruitment sites that will screen
candidates for a fraction of the cost involved in using a headhunter. As a
result, many executive recruiters feel vulnerable to the new economics of

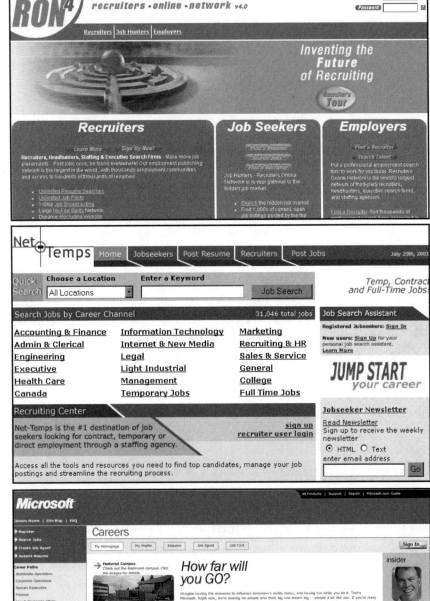

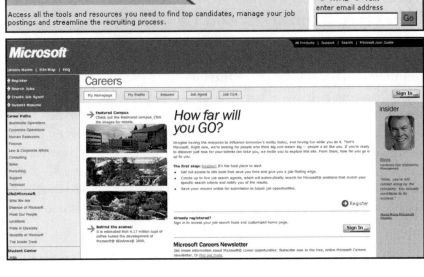

Internet recruitment. In their quest for resumes, executive recruiters are frequent users of online resume databases. They also post numerous job listings as well as register to receive "free" resumes from the many resume-blasting firms outlined in Chapter 9 (pages 131-134).

The old days when candidates were told not to contact executive recruiters – they will contact you if interested – are largely gone. In this new era of online recruitment, it's incumbent upon you to get your resume into all the right hands, which means recruiters. If you make in excess of $50,000 a year, you may want to explore several of these websites. While some sites are designed for executive-level candidates, other sites focus on recruiting individuals with high-demand skill sets. Some of these sites, such as Netshare, ExecuNET, and ExecutiveOnly, reverse the revenue model by charging job seekers membership fees to use their sites but allowing employers and recruiters to use them free of charge. As you will quickly discover, executives earning $100,000+ a year tend to pay more for everything, from site memberships to resume-blasting, assessment, counseling, and coaching services.

The following sites are disproportionately operated by recruiters or designed for executive-level candidates and recruiters.

Oya's Directory of Recruiters   **Recruiters**
www.i-recruit.com

This is one of the Internet's best sites for locating recruiters. Free to both job seekers and recruiters, this site's database includes thousands of recruiters classified into 13 major categories:

- Agriculture
- Art and Media
- Communications
- Computers & IT
- Engineering
- Finance
- Health
- Home
- Industrial
- Legal
- Professional
- Science
- Travel

If you want to target recruiters in a particular professional field, use this site to search for them by specialty and send them your resume. Most recruiters welcome resumes by indicating the types of skill sets they need and including their email addresses and telephone and fax numbers. You also can search for recruiters by location, including international recruiters. A great site for exploring the "hidden job market" of recruiters.

Chief Monster.com   **Recruiter**
http://my.chief.monster.com

This senior executive site of Monster.com is free and confidential for job seekers who are seeking senior-level opportunities with major employers, executive search firms, and venture capitalists. Both job seekers and employers are required to join this site in order to use its many services. Job seekers must meet certain experience and salary qualifications in order to participate in the site. This includes a resume database, job listings, networking opportunities, and useful articles for job seekers. Before paying monthly membership fees to other executive recruiting sites, be sure to explore the free opportunities available through this site.

Recruiters Online Network   **Recruiter**
www.recruitersonline.com

Job seekers can view job postings online as well as post their resumes on this site for free. Includes a section for locating professional search firms in over 150 specialties and geographic areas. Over 8,000 registered recruiters, executive search firms, staffing companies, and headhunters use this site. Employers and recruiters pay monthly fees for using this site, which also includes broadcasting their job postings to over 1,500 other websites.

---

6 FigureJobs   **Recruiter**
www.sixfigurejobs.com

Designed for experienced professionals, this $100,000+ site invites executive-level candidates to post their resumes online as well as explore job postings of their client companies. You must become a member in order to use this site. However, unlike similar executive-level sites, membership for job seekers is free. Includes several career resources, such as resume writing and blasting services, which are basically sponsored links and service vendors. Includes featured companies and a listing of upcoming career events relevant to members.

ExecutivesOnly	Recruiter
www.executivesonly.com	

Focusing on executives with an annual earnings potential of $70,000 to $1+ million, this site includes numerous job postings by employers and recruiters. Its revenue model is very different from 99 percent of other employment-related websites. While most sites are supported by employers and recruiters and free to job seekers, this one is just the opposite – free to employers and recruiters but costs job seekers membership fees to use it: $155 for 14 weeks; $189 for 24 weeks (most popular); $259 for 36 weeks; and $379 for 48 weeks. The site also offers a premium resume service with a 14-week membership ($495) as well as other fee-based services (company research and resume distribution).

Netshare	Recruiter
www.netshare.com	

This award-winning executive-level site is designed to connect executive job seekers ($100,000+) with companies and recruiters. Includes a resume database and nearly 2,000 executive job listings provided by executive recruiters and companies as well as special free services for job seekers (newsletter and resume critique). Individuals must register and pay monthly membership fees in order to use this site. These range from $37.50 per month to $395 for 12 months, depending on the category of membership.

ExecuNet	Recruiter
www.execunet.com	

Focusing on $100,000+ executive-level candidates, this popular site primarily offers job postings to potential candidates. This is a no-cost service to employers and recruiters who list positions. Job seekers pay membership fees to access the services of this site: 90

days for $150; 180 days for $219; and 360 days for $399. Members receive a free resume review, access to the job database and hundreds of recruiters and companies, job search tips, research tools, a newsletter, and local networking opportunities. However, you can access the networking opportunities, which are primarily listings of upcoming breakfast meetings and cocktail parties sponsored by ExecuNet and many other organizations, without being a member. Nonmembers also can access other free sections of this site that deal with career resources or what they call "Knowledge." Like a few other membership sites that charge job seekers for proprietary online services, we have no idea as to the relative effectiveness of this site compared to sites, such as Chief Monster.com, 6FigureJobs, and Recruiters Online Network, that are free to job seekers.

Management Recruiters International   Recruiter
www.brilliantpeople.com

Operated by one of the world's largest executive recruitment firms, this site includes three major sections:

- Search for Jobs
- Find a Recruiter
- Manage Your Career

All the listed jobs and recruiters are part of MRI's network, which includes more than 1,000 offices and 5,000 search professionals in North America, Europe, and Asia with total billings over $570 million – one of the largest and most active recruitment firms. It's also part of a large workplace solutions company with $1.7 billion in annual billings (www.cdicorp.com). This site also includes useful career tools for assessing skills, improving resumes, and acquiring salary (www.salary.com) and relocation information (www.realtor.com). Its career resources section includes tips on resumes, interviews, career counselors, and working with a recruiter.

| **ResumeZapper** | **Recruiter** |
| **www.resumezapper.com** | |

This is one of the largest and most active resume-blasting firms that only works with third-party recruiters, headhunters, and search firms. Candidates who prefer using executive recruiters for locating employers pay this company $49.95 to blast their resume to thousands of top search, recruitment, and placement firms. Just go online with your credit card and resume and within a few hours your resume will be in the hands of key third-party recruiters who may contact you within 48 hours about possible job openings in your area of expertise. If you're lucky, you may soon be interviewing for a job you may not have found by other means. A quick and inexpensive way to get your resume into hands of individuals who claim to know how to market you to their clients.

Other useful websites with a decided emphasis on recruiters and executive-level candidates include:

- **Kennedy Information**   www.kennedyinfo.com
                                            www.executiveagent.com
- **Heidrick & Struggles**   www.heidrick.com
- **Korn/Ferry International**   www.ekornferry.com
                                            www.futurestep.com
- **Lucas Group**   www.lucascareers.com
- **Recruit USA**   www.recruitusa.com
- **Spencer Stuart**   www.spencerstuart.com

For additional resume-blasting services designed for reaching recruiters, see our listing of several such firms in the resume distribution section of Chapter 9.

Staffing and Employment Firms

Thousands of staffing and employment firms provide placement services for part-time, full-time, and contract employees. In the Washington, DC area, for example, over 200 such firms compete for this lucrative staffing

business. Employers normally contact these firms for identifying qualified
candidates. The firms screen candidates as well as offer a variety of
personnel services and hiring options to employers. If you're interested in
getting your resume into the databases of these firms, you might start
with the following companies, which have a large presence in the staffing
industry. Many of these firms specialize in particular occupational fields
and industries.

| Net-Temps | Staffing Firms |
| www.net-temps.com | |

This is one of the Internet's top employment sites designed for
three groups: job seekers, recruiters, and employers. It specializes
in contract and temporary employment. Individuals can post
resumes online and review job postings relating to their occupation. See Chapter 5 (page 70) for more information on Net-Temps.

| Robert Half International | Staffing Firms |
| www.rhii.com | |

This is one of the world's largest staffing agencies specializing in
the fields of accounting and finance, administrative support,
information technology, law, advertising, marketing, and web
design. See Chapter 11 (pages 153) for more information on this
firm.

| Manpower | Staffing Firms |
| www.manpower.com | |

This is the world's largest staffing firm with over 3,700 offices and
franchises in 63 countries around the world. Manpower has more
than 1,200 offices in North America. It literally places over 2
million candidates each year for part-time and full-time positions.
Since individuals become employees of Manpower, which sends
them on job assignments, they acquire a certain level of job sta-
bility normally associated with large well established and growing
firms. Using an online upload form, job seekers can apply to
Manpower by submitting their resume to 10 different Manpower

offices. The firm's innovative Global Learning Center is designed to help its employees upgrade their skills online by offering more than 100 business skills courses and over 1,000 software and IT courses.

| **Kelly Services** | **Staffing Firms** |
| **www.kellyservices.com** | |

This well established staffing services firm, and Fortune 500 company, operates offices in 26 countries around the world. It places nearly 700,000 employees with more than 200,000 employers each year. Individuals can register online by uploading their resume or "Profile" (site also includes tips on composing and sending such a resume).

| **Olsten Staffing Services** | **Staffing Firms** |
| **www.olsten.com** | |

This is another large player in the staffing industry. Offers temporary, temp-to-hire, and full-time job opportunities with their many corporate and government clients. The website is very dated, with many links that have been extinct for several years. The site includes a searchable database of Olsten offices which visitors are asked to contact for more information on opportunities.

Model Employer Sites

One of the most important employment trends today is the continuing development of sophisticated employer websites, which include special employment sections with job boards, resume databases, and job tips. As noted in Chapter 9, more and more employers encourage applicants to visit their website in order to become better acquainted with the company, explore employment opportunities, and apply for jobs online. Such websites save both the company and applicants a great deal of time and money by improving the speed and quality of the whole screening process. As more and more companies develop such functional websites, fewer employers will use the many mega employment websites outlined in Chapter 5. Indeed, smaller companies, which do not have a great deal of visibility with job seekers, are most likely to use the online recruitment services of these mega sites.

Most employers maintain an employment section on their website, which usually appears on the homepage. Depending on the size and employment needs of a company, this section may include the latest job openings as well as a resume database into which a visitor can enter his or her resume. Some company websites also include profiles of current employees, insights into the company culture, and relatively frank tips on how to best write a resume and interview for jobs with the company. Many sites now include self-tests for determining whether or not a candidate would fit well into the company culture.

There are literally hundreds of thousands of such employer websites on the Internet. If you are interested in targeting particular employers, you are well advised to identify employers for which you would like to work, explore their website for employment information, and respond to relevant online job listings and/or enter your resume into their resume database. Here are two excellent examples of employer websites which include a wealth of employment information:

Boston Consulting Group   Employer
www.bcg.com/careers/careers_splash.jsp

The Boston Consulting Group is one of the world's major consulting groups and one of the best places to work. It attracts the top talent from America's top universities. If you're interested in working for BCG, be sure to explore their "Careers @ BCG" section. More than most other company websites, BCG's includes a wealth of job search information, from career tracks (there is basically one), profiles of personnel (very informative), and information on virtual project teams, to interview preparation and online applications. It also includes information on life after BCG, including associates, consultants, and alumni. The interview section is useful for any job seeker, since it deals with case interviews, interactive cases, brain teasers, and questions likely to be asked in a BCG interview. This site also includes a link to Wetfeet.com for a special report on BCG. For an employer website, it simply does not get much better than BCG. Indeed, this may be a model for other employer websites in the future.

Microsoft   Employer
www.microsoft.com/jobs/

When was the last time you saw Microsoft advertising for candidates? You won't find this company using job boards to recruit
candidates. They don't have to. Microsoft literally receives hundreds, and sometimes thousands, of unsolicited resumes each day.
In order to best manage the resume intake and screening processes,
Microsoft maintains a separate "Jobs" section on its website. This
section provides a good overview of life at Microsoft (campus,
culture, diversity, benefits), information on its locations in the
United States and abroad, career paths, and related job information. Job seekers can submit their resume online as well as search
online job listings and apply for specific jobs. The site also includes
feature articles, a careers newsletter, student center, and lots of
information on the company, its employees, and benefits. In many
respects, this is a model recruitment site for a large corporation
that has an excellent word-of-mouth reputation as being a great
place to work. Since Microsoft is able to meet many of its personnel needs just through the operation of this section on their website, you may not find many Microsoft positions listed in the many
websites outlined in this book. In other words, if you want to work
for Microsoft, go directly to the "Jobs" section on their site and
follow the application and database instructions.

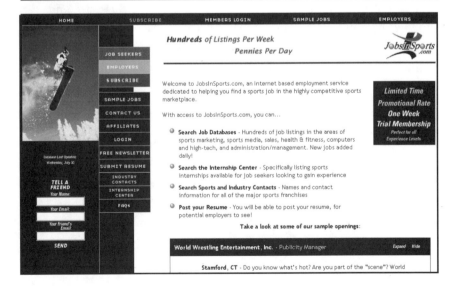

14

Specialty Occupational and Job Sites

W HILE MANY OF THE MEGA employment sites identified in Chapter 5 may include job postings and resume databases related to your occupational interests, numerous other sites specialize in particular occupational fields. Often referred to as "niche" or "boutique" employment sites, these are very focused websites. Employers and recruiters increasingly use these sites because they are more likely to attract the types of candidates they are looking for than the more general mega employment sites. Best of all for job seekers, these niche sites include lots of useful information on their profession, from special news features to networking opportunities with fellow professionals.

Finding Your Specialty

The sites featured in this chapter represent a few of many employment websites that primarily focus on specific occupational fields. If your field is not represented here, we recommend using the search engines identified in Chapter 2, such as www.google.com or the meta search engine 1-Page Multi Search (www.bjorgul.com), to find additional sites related to your occupational interests. At the same time, you should visit several of the mega employment websites outlined in Chapter 5. Monster.com, as well as a few other sites, operate specialty occupational sites. You also should review the websites of professional associations related to your occupational interests. Many of these associations operate placement services and online databases for linking job seekers with employers. For quick online access to these groups, check out Associations on the Net for identifying your relevant professional associations:

www.ipl.org/div/aon

Academia and Education

Numerous websites focus on job opportunities for educators. Over 80 percent of these sites are found within professional academic associations or focus on particular disciplines, such as library science, physics, and mathematics. You may want to first explore the career or employment sections of your professional association and then check out several education employment sites found here. Ironically, the Internet has not significantly altered the way many educational institutions hire (lengthy job descriptions with lots of formal duties and responsibilities and application requirements involving a curriculum vitae, three letters of recommendation, and perhaps samples of articles written or copies of teaching evaluations). With a few exceptions, this employment sector is still primarily wedded to the traditional print job announcement that usually goes into the placement section of their professional association's magazine or newspaper. The following websites are well worth visiting for uncovering employment opportunities in education at all levels, from teaching to administration.

Academic360.com	**Academia**
www.academic360.com	

This site represents a meta-collection of websites for the academic hunter. It includes links to HR announcements at nearly 1,800 colleges and universities in the U.S., Canada, Australia, and the United Kingdom. It also links to faculty and administrative listings at various institutions as well as faculty and administrative position announcements by discipline found with professional associations.

Chronicle of Higher Education   Academia
http://chronicle.com/jobs

If you are in academia – faculty, administrative, executive, or nonacademic position – you'll want to make this one of your first Internet stops. After all, most major colleges and universities routinely post their job announcements with *The Chronicle of Higher Education* and none age beyond 30 days. This site includes hundreds of traditional job listings which also appear in the print edition of *The Chronicle of Higher Education*. While the site does not offer a resume database, it does include a keyword search function, an email alert option, career news, salary surveys (averages by institution and rank), articles, advice, discussion forums, and more. Recent articles dealt with the treacherous nature of the academic job market. This is a great site for career information, but it does not make full use of Internet recruitment technology, especially given the absence of a resume database.

HigherEdJobs   Academia
www.higheredjobs.com

One of the most popular academic employment sites, HigherEd Jobs claims to have over 4,097 faculty and staff positions at more than 712 colleges and universities in its database. Job seekers can search positions by academic category (administrative/staff, executive, faculty, part-time/adjunct) and location (state/province or institution). Individuals can post their resumes online, receive job announcements by email, and track their applications.

Education America Network   Academia
www.educationamerica.net

This is a very user-friendly site that allows job seekers to post resumes online and search for positions by category and location. Covers all types of educational institutions. Allows users to browse for employers. Includes a useful resource section (state certification and salary information and job search tips on resumes, cover letters, and interviews) and an international education section.

K-12Jobs   **Education**
www.k12jobs.com

This no-frills site does exactly what you might expect – includes a large job posting section where job seekers can view available opportunities at kindergartens, elementary schools, junior high schools, high schools, and vocational schools. Job seekers also can post their resumes online. The site includes sections on job fairs, state certifications, education resources, resumes, salaries, news groups, and Q&A.

Academic Employment Network   **Academia**
www.academploy.com

This site covers academic positions at all levels – from primary to higher education. Allows job seekers to post their resumes online, search job listings, and review useful professional development resources. Job seekers can use the locator database, which includes over 675 school districts and universities, by paying a user fee of $19.95 for six months. They also can post their resume for a fee of $9.95 for six months. Employers pay to post positions online. Compared to most employment websites that have worked out a more user-friendly revenue model, this one seems to be a nickel-and-dime operation by charging fees at both ends – job seeker and employer.

Several additional websites also focus on teaching and other academic jobs:

- **Academic Careers Online**   www.academiccareers.com
- **Academic Position Network**   www.apnjobs.com
- **American Association of**   www.aacc.nche.edu/Template.
  Community Colleges   cfm?Section=CareerCenter
- **Carney Sandoe & Associates**   www.csa-teach.com

- C-collegeJobs.com   www.ccollegejobs.com
- Ed-U-Link   www.edulink.com
- Education Jobs   www.nationjob.com/education
- Education-Jobs.net   www.education-jobs.net
- EducationJobs.com   www.educationjobs.com
- Education World   www.educationworld.com/jobs
- ESLworldwide.com   www.eslworldwide.com
- iTeachNet (international)   www.iteachnet.com
- Jobsinschools.com   www.jobsinschools.com
- National Teacher
  Recruitment Clearinghouse   www.recruitingteachers.org
- ProTeacher   www.proteacher.com
- School Staff   www.schoolstaff.com
- Teacher Job Links   www.geocities.com/athens/
                               forum/2080
- Teacherjobsite.com   www.teacherjobsite.com
- Teachers Employment
  Network   www.teachingjobs.com
- TeachersNet   www.teachers.net/jobs
- Teacher's Planet.com   www.teachersplanet.com
- Teachers @ Work   www.teachersatwork.com
- Teachers-Teachers.com   www.teachers-teachers.com
- Teaching Jobs Overseas   www.joyjobs.com
- TeachWave   www.teachwave.com
- TEFLnetJobs   www.tefl.net/jobs
- TESOL JobFinder   www.tesol.org/careers
- The International Educator   www.tieonline.com
- USTeach.com   www.usteach.com
- WantToTeach.com   www.wanttoteach.com
- Women in Higher Education   www.wihe.com/jobs

Airline Industry

While most airlines maintain an employment section on their websites, check out these websites for job information related to the airline industry.

AirlineCareer.com   Airlines
www.airlinecareer.com

If you are interested in becoming a flight attendant, this site will help focus your job search and give you a competitive advantage in what remains a highly competitive career field. Covering 51 airlines, the site includes an online pre-qualification test and feature articles about flight attendants. It includes numerous services to help individuals become flight attendants – a career Evaluation Center, a comprehensive Application Center, an interactive Testing Center, 60 sample interview questions, pay rates for 24 major airlines, sample resumes, cover and thank-you letters, employment data on 26 major airlines, an interactive message board, numerous links to other sites, and much more. The membership fee for this site is $49.95 for one year or $59.95 for two years.

Aviation Jobs Online   Airlines
www.aviationjobsonline.com

Individuals can become members of this site by paying $9.95 a month to access its job listings, post resumes online, and receive job search tips, including sample interview questions. This site also offers special six-month ($59.98) and one-year ($79.98) rates and an occasional special. Members can access one of the following job areas: pilots and flight instructors; mechanics and avionics (maintenance); and flight attendants. Includes an extensive free section with links to numerous aviation-related employers.

Airline Employment Assistance Corps   Airlines
and AV Jobs Worldwide
www.avjobs.com

This is a very rich site for anyone seeking a job in aviation. Includes hundreds of job postings drawn from classified ads and a resume database. The site also includes job search tips, news, statistics, chat, links, education opportunities, and much more.

Individuals must become members in order to use the job search and resume services. The monthly cost is $19.95 for basic membership (job search only) or $24.95 for extended membership (job search plus resume services).

Other useful airline employment sites, which cover everyone from ground crew to flight crew, include:

- Airline Employee
  Placement Service   www.aeps.com
- Airline Job Site   www.airlinejobsite.com
- Airport Job Hub   www.airportjobhub.com
- Airport Job Kiosk   www.airportjobkiosk.com
- AviationNet   www.aviationnet.com
- Aviation Job Search   www.aviationjobsearch.com
- Find a Pilot   www.findapilot.com
- Flight Deck Recruitment   www.flightdeckrecruitment.com
- Flying Talent   www.flyingtalent.com
- Helicopter Employment   www.avemployment.com
- Jet Careers   www.jetcareers.com
- Jobs in Aviation   www.jobsinaviation.com
- Pilots Wanted   www.pilotswanted.com
- Traveljobz.net   www.traveljobz.net

Architecture

Architects have numerous job search sites from which to locate job opportunities. Two popular such sites include the following:

Architect Jobs   **Architects**
www.architectjobs.com

This site is one of the largest online sources for architect jobs. Job seekers can review online job listings as well as post their resume into the site's resume database. Includes architect salary information, an email service to automatically receive new job postings, a resume writing service, and a searchable database of recruiters specializing in architect placements.

Several sites specializing in construction jobs also include jobs for architects. Other useful employment websites for architects include the following:

- A/E/C JobBank   www.aecjobbank.com
- Craig's List   www.craigslist.org
- Just Architect Jobs   www.justarchitectjobs.com
- Landscape Architects   www.landscapearchitects.org

Arts, Entertainment, and Media

If you are in the arts, entertainment, and/or media business, you're in luck. Numerous sites focus on the diverse employment needs of several occupational groups subsumed under arts and entertainment.

Entertainment Careers   **Entertainment**
www.entertainmentcareers.net

Primarily a job bulletin board, this site allows job seekers to browse listings by position, including internships. Most jobs are found in Southern California. The site maintains regional sites for New York, Northern California, and Chicago. Includes the telephone numbers of job hotlines of the major studios and networks (under "Job Lines") as well as salary information in television and radio.

ShowBizJobs.com   **Entertainment**
www.showbizjobs.com

This is a highly functional site for job seekers in the entertainment business. Job seekers can browse job listings by region, job category, minimum salary, company, and date. They also can search by keyword for full-time, part-time, and contract jobs. A career resource section, which includes free and fee-based (Premium Service at $35.00 for six months) services, offers chat and message boards, networking opportunities, email, industry news, bookstore, salary comparables, lists of headhunters, company research, and job placement agency recommendations.

Hollywood Web   Entertainment
www.hollywoodweb.com

This is a talent search and casting center for directors, actors, actresses, writers, technicians, models, extras, and other professionals involved in the entertainment industry. It primarily showcases talent – individuals include their publicity photos and summarize their backgrounds in the hope of attracting employers. Most job seekers will want to visit the "Post a job/Find a gig" section – a jobs board that includes information on who's hiring whom for upcoming TV and film productions.

Art Job Online   Arts
www.artjob.org

This site allows job seekers in the visual arts to search for full- and part-time employment, internships, grants, public art projects, and residencies by region, art discipline, and type of organization. The site also includes featured articles and links to other sites ("Related Sites") that provide job search assistance on everything from assessing skills and writing resumes to interviewing and negotiating salary. Job seekers must register and pay fees for accessing the job postings – $25 for three months, $40 for six months, and $75 for one year.

Other useful websites focusing on jobs in arts and entertainment include:

- **440 International (Radio)** www.440int.com
- **AM/FM Jobs** www.amfmjobs.com
- **Aquent** www.portfolio.skill.com
- **Artist Resource** www.artistresource.org/jobs.htm
- **Arts Resume Resources** www.wwar.com/employment-resume
- **ArtSource** www.artsource.com
- **Entertainment Job Search** www.dnaproductions.com/jobs.htm

- Gigslist.org   www.gigslist.org
- HollywoodWeb   www.hollywoodweb.com
- Medialine   www.medialine.com
- Media Jobz   www.mediajobz.com
- MediaRecruiter   www.mediarecruiter.com
- National Association of
  Broadcasters Career Center   www.nab.org/bcc
- Playbill Online   www.playbill.com/jobs/find
- Temp Art   www.tempart.com
- TVandRadioJobs.com   www.tvandradiojobs.com
- TVJobs.com   www.tvjobs.com

Business

In many respects, most of the mega employment sites outlined in Chapter 5 focus on business. However, many segments of the business community operate their own specialized sites. Some of them are connected to professional business associations while others are operated by entrepreneurs and headhunters. Here is a sampling of some of the best business sites.

Careers in Business	Business
www.careers-in-business.com	

This site functions as a gateway to jobs in various business-related fields: accounting, consulting, finance, marketing, and nonprofit. Includes summaries of fields, recommended readings, links to online resources, and websites specializing in the particular career field. It's especially appropriate for someone interested in exploring different business fields or just embarking on a career in business.

Bank Jobs	Banking
www.bankjobs.com	

During the past 10 years, banking has become one of the most volatile career fields with numerous institutions closing, cutting back, or merging with other banks. This site provides job search services to banking and financial services specialists. Individual job seekers can post their resume online as well as search a database of job listings. The site includes banking news features, bank profiles, and links to many other banking and career resource sites.

Benefitslink.com   **Business**
http://benefitslink.com/jobs/index.shtml

If you are in the benefits field, this is the site for you. It's very small and narrowly focused. And there's nothing fancy about this site – employers post "help wanted" ads and candidates post their resumes. The goal is simple – connect the two! The jobs can be searched by date, title, location, and employer; candidates can be searched by date, title, and state. You also can sign up for the free, confidential benefits-jobs mailing list. Includes a database of over 2,000 candidates and 200 jobs.

Telecom Careers   **Telecom**
www.telecomcareers.net

If you are in the telecommunications field, this site may be able to put you in contact with your next employer. Includes the standard online resume database and job postings. Job seekers can search for jobs by keyword, industry category, and location. The site also allows job seekers to set up a Telecom Search Agent, create an "in box" to store interesting jobs, and use several online career resources. The site includes a career center, training center, news, dictionary (to look up telecommunications terminology and abbreviations), bookstore, and a stock market center.

Accountant Jobs   **Accounting**
www.accountantjobs.com

Includes numerous job postings for job seekers as well as an online resume database for employers. Job seekers can elect to have new job postings automatically emailed to them. Offers online resume writing/revising assistance (fee-based) and links to its more than 225 other eJobstore sites (organized by occupational field).

Financial Jobs   Finance
www.financialjobs.com

This award-winning site includes a wealth of job search information for individuals seeking jobs in accounting and finance. In addition to its numerous job postings and resume database, the site includes expert advice, articles, and resources for improving one's job search and resume. Includes links to several other sites that provide career and relocation assistance, such as www.distinctiveweb.com and www.homefair.com.

Jobs4Sales   Sales
www.jobs4sales.com

This is one of the best online sites for sales and marketing jobs, and is also part of the LocalCareers.com network. Job seekers can post their resume online as well as search for job listings. They can search for jobs by keywords, location, categories, and job class (from contract to full time). Includes numerous job search tips by career experts on resumes, interviews, and career fairs as well as links to other online job resources and sites with classified ads.

For additional examples of business-related employment websites, we recommend examining the directory listings available through these two gateway career sites:

- **AIRS Job Board Directory**   www.airsdirectory.com/directories/job_boards
- **Quintessential Careers**   www.quintcareers.com

Computers and Information Technology

This is one of the largest categories of employment websites with literally hundreds of specialized sites focusing on high-tech jobs. Many of the sites are very narrowly focused around specific applications, such as Oracle and UNIX, new media, web design, telecom, and specific hardware and software. These also are some of the best designed sites since they showcase the talents of computer and IT professionals. The following sites are just a small sampling of more than 1,000 specialized computer and IT employment websites:

DICE   **Computers/IT**
www.dice.com

This is one of the most popular websites for IT professionals interested in permanent, contract, and consulting jobs. It's also a popular site for both employers and recruiters in search of talent. The site includes over 25,000 high-tech jobs which users can search by keywords, skills, job titles, locations, and zip codes. While this is primarily a job posting site, it does allow job seekers to store their resume online, automatically receive new job postings by email, subscribe to a free career newsletter, and use several online job search tools and career resources. DICE's annual salary survey should be of special interest to job seekers.

Computer Jobs   **Computers**
www.computerjobs.com

This is one of the largest (1.2 million registered users and 350,000 IT resumes) and most popular websites for job seekers in the computer field. Includes a database of over 6,500 jobs in seven specialty areas. Job seekers can post their resumes on this site as well as search for jobs by location and keywords. Includes numerous useful career resources, such as career assessment, resume services, publications, user groups, and training events. Its annual salary survey is of special interest to anyone attempting to keep abreast of salary comparables in this fast-paced field.

Computer Work   **Computers/IT**
www.computerwork.com

Job seekers can enter their resume in the site's database and search for job postings by keywords, skills, job titles, or locations. The site includes more than 300,000 IT candidates in its resume database and posts over 9,000 current jobs. It includes a "Family of Sites" for 48 different locations (cities and states) and skills sets (UNIX, Networking, C++, Java, Windows, Oracle, and 10 other applications).

Many other websites also focus on job opportunities in computers and information technology:

- AwesomeTechs.com   www.awesometechs.com
- Brainbench   www.brainbench.com
- Brainpower   www.brainpower.com
- Brainbuzz   www.brainbuzz.com
- Brassring (see Chapter 5) www.brassring.com
- CareerShopIT   www.it.careershop.com
- EmploymentGuide
  (see Chapter 5)   www.employmentguide.com
- ComputerScience Jobs   www.computersciencejobs.com
- Craig's List   www.craigslist.org
- DatabaseJobs.com   www.databasejobs.com
- Hire Strategy   www.hirestrategy.com
- Hot Tech Careers   www.hottechcareers.com
- IT Careers.com   www.itcareers.com
- IT Talent   www.ittalent.com
- Jobs4IT   www.jobs4it.com
- JustASPJobs   www.justaspjobs.com
- Operation IT   www.operationit.com
- Search Database   www.searchdatabase.
                            techtarget.com
- Techies.com   www.techies.com

Construction

The construction industry includes a wide range of jobs, from construction manager and carpenter to plumber and welder. The following sites include a wide variety of construction positions for numerous types of construction industries. Many of the sites focusing on architects, engineers, and real estate also deal with construction.

Construction Jobs   **Construction**
www.constructionjobs.com

One of the primier sites in the construction, building, and design industries. Allows job seekers to post their resumes online and search for job listings relevant to more than 100 construction-related positions. Individuals can post their resumes free of charge to multiple construction industries and job titles. Employers pay subscription fees to post jobs and access the resume database. Includes a useful career center with information and advice on resume writing, interviewing, relocation, salary, job hunting, continuing education, and industry resources.

Construction Job Store   **Construction**
www.constructionjobstore.com

This site allows users to post their resumes and review current job openings in construction search jobs by job title, company, and keyword. Includes employer profiles, an automatic email option, salary information, and links to related families of websites. Primarily functions as a job bank.

Other construction-related sites worth visiting include the following:

■ Architect Jobs	www.architectjobs.com
■ Carpenter Jobs	www.carpenterjobs.com
■ Construction Gigs	www.constructiongigs.com
■ Construction Manager Jobs	www.constructionmanager job.com
■ Construction Work Jobs	www.constructionworkjobs.com
■ Electrician Jobs	www.electricianjobs.com
■ Engineer Employment	www.engineeremployment.com
■ Estimator Jobs	www.estimatorjobs.com
■ Find a Sub	www.findasub.com
■ iHire Construction	www.ihireconstruction.com
■ Jobsite	www.jobsite.com
■ New Home Sales Jobs	www.newhomesalesjobs.com

- Plumber Jobs   www.plumberjobs.com
- Project Manager Jobs   www.projectmanagerjobs.com
- Trade Jobs Online   www.tradejobsonline.com

Engineering

Engineering is a very broad and diverse field encompassing a large variety of engineers. The following websites connect the employment world of engineers.

EngineeringJobs   **Engineering**
www.engineeringjobs.com

This is a rich site for job seekers who can post their resumes online and explore numerous employment resources. Includes alphabetical listings of engineering firms, recruiters, and headhunters, along with contact information and links. Its sister site, www.contract engineering.com, is designed for individuals seeking contract, rather than permanent, work. Offers a fee-based ($35) resume distribution service that will blast your resume to 700 headhunters and recruiting firms specializing in engineering and high-tech jobs. Includes links to several professional associations of engineers, many of which have their own job banks.

EngineerEmployment   **Engineering**
www.engineeremployment.com

Another site which is part of the www.ejobstores.com family of employment websites. Includes a resume database and job postings along with employer profiles and an automatic email notification option (Job Search Agent). Includes a special salary information section for engineers.

Other engineering sites, which tend to specialize in particular types of engineers, include:

- **Biomedical Engineer**   www.biomedicalengineer.com
- **Chemical Engineer**   www.chemicalengineer.com

- Chemical Engineer Jobs   www.chemicalengineerjobs.com
- Civil Engineer Jobs   www.civilengineerjobs.com
- Contract Engineering   www.contractengineering.com
- Craig's List   www.craigslist.org
- Engineering-jobs-here   www.engineering-jobs-here.com
- Environmental Engineer   www.environmentalengineer.com
- Industrial Engineer   www.industrialengineer.com
- Manufacturing Engineer   www.manufacturingengineer.com
- Mechanical Engineer   www.mechanicalengineer.com
- Network Engineer   www.networkengineer.com
- Petroleum Engineer   www.petroleumengineer.com
- Sales Engineer   www.salesengineer.com
- Semiconductor Engineer   www.semiconductorengineer.com
- Software Engineer   www.softwareengineer.com

Health Care

Health care is one of today's fastest growing employment arenas. As hospitals and other health care providers scramble to meet continuing demand for talented employees, more and more health care-related websites have evolved to meet their needs. Several sites specialize in particular health care occupations, such as physician, nurse, hospital, radiology, dental, allied health, and emergency medicine.

Monster Healthcare   **Healthcare**
http://healthcare.monster.com

Another well organized site operated by Monster.com. In addition to job postings and a resume database, this site includes a rich collection of informative articles, career resources, a message board, educational opportunities, licensing boards, and more.

MedHunters.com   **Healthcare**
www.medhunters.com

This site allows job seekers to post resumes and search job listings in all health care specialties. Its database includes nearly 20,000 job postings and more than 900 hospitals and employers. Special features include featured employers and location, career resources, short term/seasonal employment, tutorials, frequently asked questions, tips on telephone interviews, and more. The "Professions" section includes valuable information on job postings, licensing requirements, professional organizations, education, contact information, and visa and immigration assistance for 30 health care professions and students.

MedCAREERS	Healthcare
www.medcareers.com	

Job seekers can post resumes and search online job listings, which number over 20,000. This site also includes company profiles and offers a few useful job search resources which are mainly articles. Not all resource links are up-to-date and active.

Health Care Jobs USA	Healthcare
www.healthcarejobsusa.com	

Representing a small community within the health care industry, this health care employment site specializes on job opportunities for Occupational Therapists, Physical Therapists, and Speech Therapists. It includes numerous job postings organized by field and location. Offers continuing education courses, online workshops, a message board for Q&A and networking, and links to other relevant websites.

Numerous other health-related websites offer job opportunities for a large range of occupational specialties:

- 4 MD Jobs.com   www.4mdjobs.com
- 4 Nursing Jobs.Com   www.4nursingjobs.com
- Allied Health Employment www.gvpub.com
- CompHealth   www.comphealth.com
- Dentist Jobs   www.dentistjobs.com
- DentSearch   www.dentsearch.com
- PhyJob   www.phyjob.com
- Echo-Web   www.echocareers.com

- e-Dental — www.e-dental.com
- Health Care Jobs Online — www.hcjobsonline.com
- Health Care Recruiters — www.hcrecruiters.com
- Health Care Jobs (book) — www.healthcarejobs.org
- Health Care Job Store — www.healthcarejobstore.com
- Health Care Recruitment — www.healthcarerecruitment.com
- Health Care Source — www.healthcaresource.com
- Health Care Talents — www.healthcaretalents.com
- Health Care Works — www.healthcareworks.org
- Health CareerWeb — www.healthcareerweb.com
- Health Jobsite.com — www.healthjobsite.com
- Healthlinks.net — www.healthlinks.net
- Health Network USA — www.hnusa.com
- Health Opps — www.healthcare.careerbuilder.com
- HIPjobs.net — www.HIPjobs.net
- Hospitalhub.com — www.hospitalhub.com
- Hospital Jobs Online — www.hospitaljobsonline.com
- Hospital Jobs USA — www.hospitaljobsusa.com
- iHireNursing — www.ihirenursing.com
- iHirePhysicians.com — www.ihirephysicians.com
- Job Health Careers — www.jobhealthcareers.net
- Jobscience — www.jobscience.com
- MD Direct.com — www.mddirect.com
- MDJobSite.com — www.mdjobsite.com
- Med Options — www.medoptions.com
- Medical Sales Jobs — www.medicalsalesjobs.com
- MedJobs2000 — www.medjobs2000.com
- Medjump — www.medjump.com
- MedSearch — www.medsearch.com
- MedZilla — www.medzilla.com
- Nursejobz — www.nursejobz.com
- Nurse-Recruiter.com — www.nurse-recruiter.com
- Nursing Spectrum — www.nursingspectrum.com
- Pharmaceutical Rep Jobs — www.pharmaceuticalrepjobs.com
- PhysicianBoard — www.physicianboard.com
- Physicians Employment — www.physemp.com
- Practice Choice — www.practicechoice.com
- RTJobs.com — www.rtjobs.com

- Ultrasoundjobs.com   www.ultrasoundjobs.com
- Vital Careers   www.vitalcareers.com

Hospitality and Travel

Despite recent (2001-2003) downturns due to a combination of international terrorism and recession, the hospitality and travel industry is one of the largest and fastest growing industries in the world. It's also a truly global industry with millions of jobs available at home and abroad. Compared to most industries, this one tends to offer a very high level of job satisfaction. As long as economies grow, this sector of the job market should experience continuing growth.

While most major hospitality providers (hotels, resorts, restaurants, chefs, caterers, amusement parks, bars, convention centers, spas, travel agencies and operators, rail services, corporate travel managers, convention and meeting planners, tourist promotion offices, car rental companies, cruise lines, clubs, casinos) maintain their own websites with employment information, numerous other websites focus on supplying a fascinating range of talent to various sectors of this industry, from chefs (www.chefjob.com and www.chefnet.com) to gentlemen hosts (www.the workingvacation.com).

Hospitality Adventures **www.hospitalityadventures.com**	**Hospitality**

This is a major meeting place where employers and candidates in the hospitality industry meet, especially for hotel, resort, restaurant, casino, club, and cruise ship positions. Includes an online resume database and job listings, featured employers, and links to numerous related clubs and organizations, colleges and universities, employment resources, publications, and state associations.

Hospitality Careers Online **www.hcareers.com**	**Hospitality**

Focusing on the restaurant and hospitality industry, this very focused site basically does two things – allows job seekers to post their resumes online and search job postings and offers employers and recruiters the opportunity to access the resume database and advertise their opportunities online. Job seekers can search jobs by industry, position, management level, domestic and international locations, and keywords. Also includes employer profiles, links to professional organizations and services, career resources, hospitality programs at universities and colleges, and linkages to their separate sites for Canada and the United Kingdom/Ireland. Just for fun, check out the hilarious observations found under the "Unique Sites" section (see "Links").

Job Monkey.com   **Hospitality**
www.jobmonkey.com

This friendly and colorful site allows job seekers to upload their resume or profile online as well as search and apply for jobs online. An especially appealing site for young people just starting a career or those looking for seasonal or part-time work in "cool" hospitality and travel jobs. Includes special coverage of jobs with Alaska fisheries, cruise lines, outdoors, airlines and airports, land tours, casinos and gaming, resorts, ski industry, and teaching abroad. The site is rich with resources, linkages, and special features. It also includes a travel center and a message board.

Numerous other websites focus on jobs and careers in the hospitality and travel industry. Some of the most interesting employment-related websites for this industry include:

- Action Jobs   www.actionjobs.com
- AirlineCareer.com   www.airlinecareer.com
- Airline Employee
  Placement Service   www.aeps.com
- Airline Employment
  Assistance Corps   www.aeac.net
- Airline Job Site   www.airlinejobsite.com
- Airport Job Hub   www.airportjobhub.com
- Airport Job Kiosk   www.airportjobkiosk.com
- AviationNet   www.aviationnet.com
- Aviation Information
  Resources   www.jet-jobs.com

- Aviation Job Search   www.aviationjobsearch.com
- AviationJobsOnline   www.aviationjobsonline.com
- Casino Careers Online   www.casinocareers.com
- Chef Job   www.chefjob.com
- Chef Jobs Network   www.chefjobsnetwork.com
- Chefs on the Net   www.chefnet.com
- CoolJobsCanada   www.cooljobscanada.com
- Cool Works   www.coolworks.com
- Cruise Jobs   www.cruisejobs.com
- Cruise Line Jobs   www.cruiselinejobs.com
- Cruise Ship Entertainment   www.cruiseshipentertainment.com
- Cruise Ship Jobs   www.shipjobs.com
- CruiseJobFinder   www.cruisejobfinder.com
- e-Hospitality.com   www.e-hospitality.com
- Entree Job Bank   www.entreejobbank.com
- Escoffier.com   www.escoffier.com
- Find a Pilot   www.findapilot.com
- Flight Deck Recruitment   www.flightdeckrecruitment.com
- Flying Talent   www.flyingtalent.com
- Food Industry Jobs.com   www.foodindustryjobs.com
- Food Management Search   www.foodmanagementsearch.com
- Foodservice Central   www.foodservicecentral.com
- Food Service.com   www.foodservice.com
- Harrison Business Group   www.harrisonbusinessgroup.com
- Helicopter Employment   www.avemployment.com
- Hospitality-1st   www.hospitality-1st.com
- Hospitality Career Net   www.hospitalitycareernet.com
- Hospitality Financial and
  Technology Professionals   www.iaha.org
- Hospitality Job Exchange   www.hprofessionals.com
- Hospitality Jobs Online   www.hjo.net
- Hospitality Link   www.hospitalitylink.com
- Hospitality Net   www.hospitalitynet.org
- Hospitality Online   www.hospitalityonline.com
- Hotel Job Resource   www.hoteljobresource.com
- Hotel Jobs (London)   www.hotel-jobs.com
- Hoteljobs.com   www.hoteljobs.com

- Hotel Jobs Network   www.hoteljobsnetwork.com
                              www.hospitalityjobs.com
- Hotel Online Classifieds   www.hotel-online.com
- Hotel Resource   www.hotelresource.com
- Hotels Hiring Online   www.hotels.hiringonline.com
- iHire Hospitality   www.ihirehospitality.com
- iHire Hospitality Services www.ihirehospitalityservices.com
- International Seafarers   www.jobxchange.com
- Jet Careers   www.jetcareers.com
- Jobs in Aviation   www.jobsinaviation.com
- Meeting Jobs   www.meetingjobs.com
- Meeting Professionals
  International   www.mpiweb.org/resources/jobs
- Outdoor Network   www.outdoornetwork.com
- Pilots Wanted   www.pilotswanted.com
- Resort Jobs   www.resortjobs.com
- Restaurant Jobs   www.restaurantjobs.com
- Restaurant Manager.net   www.restaurantmanager.net
- Restaurant Managers.Com   www.restaurantmanagers.com
- SE Hospitality   www.sehospitality.net
- Ship Center.com   www.shipcenter.com
- SkiingtheNet.com   www.skiingthenet.com
- Ski Resort Jobs   www.skiresortjobs.com
- Spa Jobs   www.spajobs.com
- Travel Jobs   www.traveljobs.com
- Traveljobz.net   www.traveljobz.net
- Workamper.com   www.workamper.com
- Working Vacation   www.theworkingvacation.com

Many of the major recruiters specializing in the hospitality industry can be found on this website:

www.hospitalityonline.com/career-links/recruiters

For more information on the many segments of the travel and hospitality industry, including hundreds of websites related to employment, see our companion book, *Jobs for Travel Lovers: Opportunities at Home and Abroad* (Impact Publications, 2003).

Law

The legal field has increasingly become more web-savvy. More and more lawyers, paralegals, and support staff now turn to the Internet for information on job opportunities in a field known for its very active "hidden job market" and "ole boy" ties. Whether you're looking for a job in law or considering a career change within the legal field, you'll find several websites to assist you with your job search. The following sites showcase thousands of job postings and resumes of individuals in the legal field.

Legalstaff   **Law**
www.legalstaff.com

Attorneys, paralegals, and other legal support staff professionals can enter their resume into the online database as well as search for jobs posted in the employer database. The site also includes tips on setting goals, writing resumes and letters, handling references, and interviewing; a salary wizard; relocation tools; and a directory of legal schools and associations. Combines the resources of 89 Legal Career Centers in this one-stop career shop.

Attorney Jobs Online   **Law**
www.attorneyjobsonline.com

Attorneys turn to this site for exploring legal and law-related jobs. Attorneys can post their resume online as well as review online job listings of employers. Individuals must subscribe to this online service – $15.00 for 30 days, $25.00 for 60 days, $37.50 for 90 days, and $75.00 for six months. Institutions can subscribe at the rate of $500.00 a year for up to two computers. The site also includes frequently asked questions, a legal search center, resume and interview advice, salary information, alternative legal careers, online career counseling, and access to The Insider's Guide to the top 140 law firms in the Washington, DC area. Other sections of the site offer information on publications, advisories, trends, opportunities for law students, attorney hot jobs, part-time and temporary attorney jobs, outplacement services, and email alerts.

> **Law.com CareerCenter**   **Law**
> **www.lawjobs.com**

This is primarily a job board for lawyers, paralegals, and support staff, which includes nearly 2,000 jobs in its database. Job seekers also can post their resumes into the site's searchable database. Includes job listings for five occupational groups: attorneys, paralegals, secretaries, administrative/ support staff, and management and technical personnel. The site also includes news articles, a directory of search firms organized by states and alphabetically, links to recruiting pages of top law firms, and several special lists that rank law firms by various criteria. Operated by American Lawyer Media Publication which includes numerous other sites.

Other useful websites for individuals in the legal fields include the following:

- 411 Legal Info — www.411legalinfo.com/JOBS
- Attorney Job Store — www.attorneyjobstore.com
- AttorneyJobs.com — www.attorneyjobs.com
- Corporate Attorney Jobs — www.corporateattorneyjobs.com
- CounselHounds.com — www.counselhounds.com
- Counsel.net — www.counsel.net
- Craig's List — www.craigslist.com.org
- eAttorney — www.eattorney.com
- Emplawyer.net — www.emplawyernet.com
- Environmentalattorneyjobs — www.environmentalattorneyjobs.com
- FindLaw Career Center — www.careers.findlaw.com
- Find Law Job.com — www.findlawjob.com
- iHire Legal — www.ihirelegal.com
- Jobs.LawInfo.com — www.jobs.lawinfo.com
- Juris Resources.com — www.jurisresources.com
- LawGuru.com — www.lawguru.com
- LawListings.com — www.lawlistings.com
- Law Match — www.lawmatch.com
- Lawyers Weekly Jobs — www.lawyersweeklyjobs.com

- LegalCV.com (UK)   www.legalcv.com
- Legal Employment   www.legalemploy.com
- LegalHire.com   www.legalhire.com
- LegalStaff.com   www.legalstaff.com
- Legal Job Store   www.legaljobstore.com
- Legal-Jobs (New York)   www.legal-jobs.com
- Litigation Attorney Jobs   www.litigationattorneyjobs.com
- NationJob Network   www.nationjob.com/legal
- Paralegal.com   paralegal.com
- Paralegal-Jobs.com   paralegal-jobs.com
                               paralegalclassifieds.com
- Paralegals.org   paralegals.org
- US Legal Jobs   uslegaljobs.com

Science

Science consists of numerous fields and specialties. Depending on your area of expertise, you should be able to find employment websites focusing on your occupational specialty. Some of the most popular science websites include the following:

BioView   **Science**
www.bioview.com

This well organized site is where top talent and employers in the biotechnology and pharmaceutical industries meet. Includes job postings and a capability to search private and public resume databases as well as search for resumes found on personal home pages and websites of professional associations and colleges. Job seekers can search jobs by discipline, location, and company. A special email feature will automatically send job postings to users who indicate a preference for receiving listings that match their profiles. Includes company profiles, company links, education resources, career resources (salary and relocation information, resume writing tips, and career links), meeting calendar, internships, and contract positions.

Science Careers   Science
http://recruit.sciencemag.org

This is the employment website of the American Association for the Advancement of Science and *Science Magazine*. It includes over 4,000 searchable job postings as well as a searchable resume database for employers. Its "Job Alerts" section automatically sends email notifications of jobs. The site also includes employer profiles, employer links, career fairs, advice and perspectives, meetings and announcements, career news, a salary survey, grants network, postdoc network, forums, articles, and academic programs. Be sure to check out the "Next Wave" section, which includes numerous job search tips and advice for scientists. A very well organized, intuitive, and informative website for job seekers. Indeed, many other employment websites could learn a lot by exploring the structure and content of this fine site.

Chemjobs   Science
www.cen-chemjobs.org

This is the official employment website of one of the world's largest professional associations of scientists, the American Chemical Society (ACS). Designed by chemists for chemists, the site includes hundreds of job postings as well as a searchable resume database for employers. The "New Job Alerts" automatically emails job seekers the latest job listings relevant to their career interests. The resource section for job seekers includes salary information, employment trends, academic employment opportunities, job search tips, career article archive, and a library of career resources, including ACS career services publications, ACS short courses, a calendar of career meetings and workshops, links to company research databases, and more. A terrific site designed to provide first-class assistance to chemists but also very useful to anyone involved in job hunting.

Other websites targeted at different groups of scientists include the following:

- Air Weather Association   www.airweaassn.org/jobs.htm
- Bio Online   http://career.bio.com
- Chemical Online   www.chemicalonline.com
- ChemistryJobs.com   www.chemistryjobs.com
- ChemJobs.net   www.chemjobs.net
- DiscoverJobs   www.discoverjobs.com
- Earthworks   www.earthworks-jobs.com
- GeoSearch   www.geosearch.com
- GeoTechJobs   www.geotechjobs.com
- JobScience.com   www.jobscience.com
- Jobs4Scientists   www.ajobs4scientists.com
- NatureJobs   www.nature.com/naturejobs
- SciJobs.org   www.scijobs.org
- WeatherJobs.com   www.weatherjobs.com

Sports and Recreation

If sports and recreation are your passions, you're in luck with the Internet. Numerous sports- and recreation-related websites offer employment opportunities relating to golf, tennis, mountain climbing, skiing, racing, sports medicine, coaching, sports broadcasting, summer camps, clubs, resorts, stadiums, arenas, high schools, colleges, women, and the outdoors. While most of the positions are full-time, many jobs, especially in resorts and summer camps, are seasonal and part-time.

JobsinSports.com   **Sports**
www.jobsinsports.com

This is a subscription-based online employment service that advertises its services under this phraseology: "Own the Hidden Job Market For Pennies a Day." Individuals pay $29.95 per month to access the site's sports job and internship listings as well as post their resume to the site's searchable Resume Bank. Employers can post to the site's employment database for free. Individuals also can post their resume to the site's database. Covers sports marketing, media, administration/management, sales, and computer/hi-tech positions. The site includes a free newsletter, sports industry contacts, and a frequently asked questions section. You can view sample job listings before deciding to subscribe to the site.

CoolWorks.com   **Recreation**
www.coolworks.com

This site includes over 75,000 jobs in its database. Job seekers can search the database as well as post their resume to the online searchable (employers) resume bank and receive weekly email updates of job postings. Includes jobs with national parks, camps, resorts and lodges, amusement parks, ski resorts, guest ranches, boats and ships, state parks, internships, and volunteering. Especially appeals to students in search of seasonal recreational employment but also includes career professional employment. Includes several useful job search resources.

GolfingCareers   **Sports**
www.golfingcareers.com

If you want to work in the golf industry, this may be the perfect site for locating job vacancies and posting your resume online. Includes several online job search tools for posting, editing, sending, and deleting a resume; searching for employers; accessing job postings; and reviewing upcoming golf events. The "19th Hole" section includes an employment resource center which links to many other job-related sites, from resume writing and relocation to recruiters and employment websites. The site also includes a list of golf associations in each state, complete with their telephone numbers and email addresses.

Other sports- and recreation-related employment sites worth exploring include the following:

- ActionJobs.com   www.actionjobs.com
- Camp Channel   www.campchannel.com/campjobs
- Camp Jobs   www.campjobs.com
- Camp Staff   www.campstaff.com
- C.O.A.C.H.   www.coachhelp.com/exe-bin/
                          loginform.cfm
- Coaching Jobs   www.coachingjobs.com

- Executive Sports Placement   www.prosportsjobs.com
- GolfSurfin   www.golfsurfin.com
- Great Summer Jobs   www.petersons.com/summerop
- JobMonkey   www.jobmonkey.com
- Monster Sports Jobs/ESPN   www.espn.monster.com
- Mountain Jobs   www.mountainjobs.com
- My Summers   www.mysummers.com
- NCAA Online   www.ncaa.org/employment.html
- OnlineSports.com   www.onlinesports.com
- Outdoor JobNet   www.outdoornetwork.com/
                               jobnetdb/index.html

- Racing Jobs   www.racingjobs.com
- SkiingtheNet.com   www.skiingthenet.com
- Ski Resort Jobs   www.skiresortjobs.com
- Sports Careers   www.1andall-sportsjobs.com
- Sports Employment   www.sportsemployment.com
- Sports Jobs For Women   www.sportsjobsforwomen.com
- Sports Medicine   www.sportsmedicinejobs.com
- Sports Workers   www.sportsworkers.com
- TeamJobs.com   www.teamjobs.com
- Tennis Jobs   www.tennisjobs.com
- Title 9 Sports   www.title9sports.com/jobs.html
- Women's Sports Careers   www.womensportsjobs.com
- Work in Sports   www.workinsports.com

15

Niche Sites for Special Job Seekers

OST OF THE JOB SITES featured or listed in Chapter 14 are relevant to specific communities of job seekers who pursue certain occupations, such as education, law, chemistry, banking, nursing, medicine, engineering, information technology, art, entertainment, travel and hospitality, accounting, architecture, construction, and sports. Individuals using these sites tend to identify with large and competitive occupational groups defined by their special skill sets.

At the same time, several communities of job seekers cut across these standard occupational groups. They have special employment needs because of their education, age, occupational status, gender, or orientation toward particular types of employment. In this chapter we feature numerous websites for these special groups.

College Students and Recent Grads

It's one of the largest and most targeted number of job seekers – college students and recent graduates. Indeed, numerous employment websites are designed to service the more than 5 million students who graduate

from college each year. Most of these sites focus on three groups of college-related job seekers:

- current students seeking internships
- soon-to-graduate students seeking full-time jobs
- recent graduates and alumni making job changes

These also can be some very volatile websites, as many sites open with high expectations but soon close because of the special challenges involved in working with this unique audience. Several sites have attempted to monopolize the college market by developing exclusive website job posting and resume database arrangements with college career centers (NACElink and MonsterTRAK) or developed specialized software for managing critical career center operations (College Central Network). Other sites are more focused on dispensing job search information and advice, operate searchable resume databases and job postings, as well as showcase employers interested in hiring students and recent graduates (CollegeGrad and CampusCareerCenter). What remain are some very well organized sites that can help college students, who are notoriously known for putting off career planning and job search decisions until the very last minute – about one or two months before graduation!

The following websites should be of special interest to college students and recent grads who need to get their act together to find a job or start a new, and hopefully rewarding, career.

CollegeGrad.com	College Students
www.collegegrad.com	

Operated by college specialist and author Brian Krueger, this popular site is rich with resources for helping college students and recent graduates find employment. In addition to offering a huge number of entry-level job postings and a searchable resume database through one of the major general sites, an added bonus of this site is the availability of the complete text of Brian's latest edition of the *College Grad Job Hunter*; it's free to read online. The most popular sections after the job postings include Resume Templates, Top 500 Entry Level Employers, and Entry Level Salaries. The site also includes a Relocation Center, Startup

Center, MBA Center, Forum, and a Job Hunter Newsletter. Rich in content, this should be a "must visit" site for all students and their parents.

CampusCareerCenter   **College Students**
www.campuscareercenter.com

This popular and informative site allows students to browse online job listings, apply for jobs, research companies, and acquire resume and interview tips. Includes numerous articles and featured employers as well as several unique elements – Ask the Expert, Career Corner, Foreign Exchange, Intern Zone, Next Step, Diversity Center, and Visa Center. Also offers several job search services, such as resume writing and loan consolidation. One of the few student sites with an international orientation by including visiting foreign national students in its scope of services. Oriented toward three audiences: students, employers, and university administrators. Students must register in order to use this site for free. Offers employers different recruitment options. A very well organized and focused site.

Job Web   **College Students**
www.jobweb.com

This is the student-oriented website of the National Association of Colleges and Employers. Since almost every college career services center belongs to this professional organization, the site reflects many of the information needs of its members. Indeed, it's one of the richest sites for career and job search information (see our earlier description on page 66). While it does not include job postings or a resume database, which are available through its sister website, www.nacelink.com, it does include articles, tips, advice, salary information, online career fairs, job market news, employer profiles, career library, and links to alumni groups, career centers, graduate schools, relocation resources, and much more. Students and employers will be especially interested in NACE's authoritative annual *Salary Survey* information on starting salaries for college graduates.

NACElink   College Students
www.nacelink.com

This is a job posting and resume site jointly sponsored by the
National Association of Colleges and Employers (NACE) and
DirectEmployers (www.directemployers.com). A direct competitor
to Monster.com's MonsterTRAK (www.jobtrak.com), it's licensed
to several member colleges and universities that use NACElink
exclusively to provide many online career services to their students
and alumni. The site allows career centers to customize the look of
the website, add their own components, and schedule interview
and information sessions. A relatively new operation, it's still in
the experimental stage as more and more colleges and universities
sign up for this program. If you are a student or college graduate,
check with your career center to see if they are using NACElink.

JobTRAK   College Students
www.jobtrak.com

This site has increasingly gone bare bones, and it's beginning to
feel the competition from NACElink. Operated by Monster.com,
this site targets college students and alumni with many of the
resources and tools available in the Monster.com job search arsenal
(see pages 59-60). It includes thousands of job listings and
internships through both Monster and affiliate college and
university career centers (most are password protected), career
advice and tips through its "Career Guide" section and a salary
center (online salary calculator and cost-of-living wizard powered
by Salary.com). You must be associated with an affiliated college
or university in order to use this site.

Other college-oriented employment sites worth examining include the
following:

- AboutJobs.com   www.aboutjobs.com
- AfterCollege.com   www.aftercollege.com
- Black Collegian   www.blackcollegian.com

- CareerBuilder — www.college.careerbuilder.com
- CcollegeJobs.com — www.ccollegejobs.com
- College Central Network — www.collegecentral.com
- CollegeJournal.com — www.collegejournal.com
- College News — www.collegenews.com/jobs.htm
- College Recruiter — www.collegerecruiter.com
- EmployU.com — www.employu.com
- Entryleveljobstore.com — www.entryleveljobstore.com
- eProNet — www.epronet.com
- Experience.com — www.experience.com
- Graduating Engineer Online — www.graduatingengineer.com
- InternJobs.com — www.internjobs.com
- InternshipPrograms.com — www.internshipprograms.com
- Internweb.com — www.internweb.com
- JobDirect.com — www.jobdirect.com
- JobMonkey.com — www.jobmonkey.com
- Kaplan, Inc. — www.kaplan.com

For more information on internships, jobs, and careers for college students, graduates, and alumni, see our recent college-to-career job search book: *The Job Hunting Guide: Transitioning From College to Career* (Impact Publications, 2003).

Military in Transition

Each year nearly 250,000 members of the U.S. military service transition to the civilian world. While some of these transitioning service members go into full-time retirement, the majority of individuals look for civilian jobs in government, business, or the nonprofit sector. Many enlisted personnel look for jobs in law enforcement, information technology, and related security and technical fields. Many junior and senior officers seek out leadership and management jobs in a variety of occupational areas. For many transitioning military personnel, this is the first time in their life that they have ever had to conduct a job search. Everything from writing a resume and networking to dressing for job interviews and negotiating salaries is new to them.

Given the special employment needs of this talented group of transitioning job seekers, several websites have been created to help them acquire basic job search skills and connect with employers who especially wish to recruit individuals with military experience. While many employers are defense contractors in need of military expertise and connections, other employers understand the value of recruiting individuals with special skills and work discipline normally associated with a military background. The following sites, as well as several websites featured in the government, nonprofit, international, and intel sections of this chapter, also are relevant to this group of job seekers.

> **Corporate Gray Online**   **Military Transition**
> **www.greentogray.com** or **www.bluetogray.com**

This unique site combines key online and offline job search products and services to help transitioning military members find employment: books, job fairs, and online job postings, resume database, and other services. Unlike most websites that use a strictly digital approach to employment, Corporate Gray Online publishes with Impact Publications annual editions of three self-directed career transition books that are given free of charge annually to 250,000 transitioning military members: *From Army Green to Corporate Gray*, *From Navy Blue to Corporate Gray*, and *From Air Force Blue to Corporate Gray*. Sponsored by employers interested in recruiting service members, the books literally provide hands-on career guidance which, in turn, are linked to a series of eight real-live job fairs. Members of the military community also can use this site to post their resumes online, browse job listings, check on upcoming job fairs, and acquire additional resources – from training and education to relocation assistance – to help with their transition. In the interests of full disclosure, we are closely associated with the writing, production, and distribution of the three books as well as providing content for this site. We believe combining both online and offline products and services – offline books and job fairs with an online database – provides one of the most powerful employment and recruitment approaches. Indeed, this is the only such employment site on the Internet that uses this unique approach to finding jobs and recruiting candidates. All products and services – books, job fairs, and website – are free to job seekers. The site also includes links to the homepages of sponsoring employers who are interested in recruiting individuals with military experience.

TAOnline	Military Transition
taonline.com	

Now part of the Lucas Group, TAOnline offers a large range of online employment services to transitioning service members, spouses, and veterans. Includes a resume database, job postings, and links to military job fairs and hiring conferences. Special sections provide useful information for spouses and dependents as well as career advice, relocation, entrepreneurship, government jobs, continuing education, military-to-civilian language translator, a jobs thesaurus, security clearances, a newsletter, and more. The site also includes contact information on all transition offices of the various services. It markets its inexpensive ($7.95 to $22.95) proprietary software products, First-Step (for students), JobMaker (for everyone), and Transition Assistance Software (for military), which can be downloaded from this site.

VetJobs.com	Military Transition
www.vetjobs.com	

This well designed site enables service members to post their resumes online, search for job postings, and explore numerous resources relevant to veterans. Special features include veteran service organizations, job search tips, veteran's and employer's newsletters, success stories, a military spouse section, forums, and links to exchanges, communities, and education services. Operated by Navy veterans dedicated to assisting fellow veterans in making job and career transitions as well as connecting to fellow members of the military community.

The Destiny Group	Military Transition
www.destinygroup.com	

One of the more entrepreneurial military transition sites, The Destiny Group enables job seekers to search for job postings by profession and location as well as post their resumes online. Includes additional services for employers and applicants, such as hiring forums, resume tools, and transition and interview advice. The Destiny Group also powers the employment sections of some other military-relevant websites, including the alumni groups of various service academies. Individuals must register to use this site.

Other websites focusing on transitioning military personnel include the following:

- **Army Times** www.armytimes.com
- **Bradley-Morris.com** www.bradley-morris.com
- **Cameron-Brooks** www.cameron-brooks.com
- **DOD Transportal** www.dodtransportal.org
- **G.I. Jobs** www.gijobs.net
- **Helmets to Hardhats** www.trades.helmetstohardhats. org
- **IntelligenceCareers.com** www.intelligencecareers.com
- **JMO Jobs** www.jmojobs.com
- **Lucas Group** www.lucascareers.com/general/ military
- **MilitaryCity.com** www.militarycity.com
- **Military.com** www.military.com
- **Military Exits** www.militaryexits.com
- **Military Headhunter** www.militaryheadhunter.com
- **MilitaryHire.com** www.militaryhire.com
- **MilitaryMatch** www.militarymatch.com
- **Military Outplacement Post** www.midwestmilitary.com
- **Military Partners** www.militarypartners.com
- **Military Transition** www.militarytransition.com
- **Military Transition Group** www.careercommandpost.com
- **Non Commission Officers Association (NCOA)** www.ncoausa.org
- **TekSystems.com** www.teksystems.com
- **The Retired Officers Association (TROA)** www.troa.org/tops
- **SmartStart for New Vets** www.smartstartvets.org

- Veterans' Employment
  and Training Service (DOL)   http:/umet-vets.dol.gov
- VeteransWorld.com   www.veteransworld.com

Executive-Level Candidates

If you expect to be making $100,000+ a year, chances are you will find
over 90 percent of the Internet employment sites irrelevant to your job
search. You have very special employment needs that are best met by
connecting with headhunters and CEOs rather than surveying job listings
and entering your resume in a mega resume database that is primarily
accessed by human resources personnel for lower level positions. Numerous websites now specialize in executive-level positions and candidates.
We outlined several of these sites in Chapter 13 (pages 171-176) when
we discussed recruiter sites. You should start with the following gateway
site to executive recruiters:

www.i-recruit.com

Individuals interested in executive-level positions are well advised to
visit the following sites. Several of them charge a monthly or quarterly
"membership" fee to access their site while others are free. We recommend starting with the free sites since they may prove to be just as
effective as the fee-based sites (we've seen no evidence to the contrary,
but you'll have to be the judge). The free sites include:

- **6 Figure Jobs**   www.sixfigurejobs.com
- **Chief Monster.com**   http://my.chief.monster.com
- **Management Recruiters
  International**   www.brilliantpeople.com
- **Recruiters Online Network** www.recruitersonline.com

Major fee-based sites for executive-level job seekers include:

- **ExecuNet**   www.execunet.com
- **ExecutivesOnly**   www.executivesonly.com
- **Netshare**   www.netshare.com

Women

If you are female, you'll find numerous websites devoted to women's employment and networking issues. As outlined in Chapter 10 (pages 139-140), the web has become a very popular place for women's networks. From an employment perspective, many women's sites are organized by professions, such as women in accountancy, journalism, communication, real estate, higher education, technology, mathematics, sports, engineering, construction, and new media. Most of these sites include a career or employment section to assist their members in finding jobs through networking and job listings. The following associations are only a few of the many professional associations of women:

- **American Society of Women Accountants**   www.aswa.org
- **Association of Women in Mathematics**   www.awm-math.org
- **Association for Women in Sports Media**   www.awsmonline.org
- **Society of Women Engineers**   www.swe.org
- **Women in Communication**   www.womcom.org
- **Women in Higher Education**   www.wihe.com
- **Women in Technology International**   www.witi.com

The following websites represent communities of women who have common professional and personal interests, with special emphasis on jobs, careers, and work issues. Most of these sites include informative job or employment sections.

iVillage	Women
www.ivillage.com	

This is the mega website for women – the largest on the Internet. Includes numerous channels that focus on a wide range of issues of interest to women – from babies to work. The "Work" section includes tips on resumes, interviews, salaries, motivation, balancing work and family, networking, getting ahead, and working from home. It also includes quizzes, news, expert advice, articles, message boards, chats, and an entrepreneur institute. Its featured sponsor, with a huge resume database and over 400,000 job postings, is www.careerbuilder.com. It even includes a "Career Astrology" link to www.career.astrology.com – just for fun or perhaps a serious approach for some job seekers who feel powerless in today's job market! A very useful site that focuses on many employment issues of special interest to women.

Career-Intelligence.com www.career-intelligence.com	Women

Dubbed *"The smart woman's online career resource,"* this site focuses on providing career tips and advice for women. It includes separate channels on assessment, job search, career management, and tools for success. The assessment section includes information on and examples of the Myers-Briggs Type Indicator®, Strong Interest Inventory®, and other assessment instruments. Includes a free newsletter, expert advice, and a separate section for freelancers and consultants.

CareerWomen www.careerwomen.com	Women

This is a full-service career site for women. Includes a resume database and job postings as well as several additional career services: corporate profiles, job search resources, career news, and expert advice. Its "CW and News Resources" section includes links to several professional associations for women in business as well as career and employment news and career development tips and articles.

Womans-Work www.womans-work.com	Women

This site is rich with employment content for women in search of life balance and flexible work situations – part-time, job share, work from home, flexible schedule, and telecommuting. Includes a job board, resume database, and job search resources. Offers a job share partner search, life balance tips, wage comparisons, interview tips, resume writing guidelines, discussion groups, resources, links, and more.

Other employment websites of special interest to women include the following:

- Advancing Women   www.advancingwomen.net
- CareerWoman2000   www.careerwoman2000.com
- Digital Women   www.digital-women.com/ work.htm
- Feminist Majority Foundation Online   www.feminist.org
- Girlgeeks   www.girlgeeks.org
- Herwebbiz.com   www.herwebbiz.com
- Jobs4Women   www.jobs4women.com
- Msmoney.com   www.msmoney.com
- Womensforum.com   www.womensforum.com
- WomensJobSite.com   www.womensjobsite.com
- Women Sports Careers   www.womensportscareers.com
- Workplace Solutions   www.workplacesolutions.org
- Work4Women   www.work4women.org

Minorities and Diversity

Minorities and diversity come in many different forms, from racial and ethnic minorities to immigrants, religious groups, gays and lesbians, women, people with disabilities, and mature workers. The following websites provide a sampling of sites that are designed to service a wide range of minorities. Most of these sites include employment opportunities.

LatPro	Minorities
www.latpro.com	

This international job site is designed for Spanish and Portuguese Speakers. Offers a wide range of job listings from many top employers. Job seekers can search for jobs by region, country, and function. Includes numerous job search resources, such as job mailing lists, relocation center, newsletters, salary expert, online English, legal advice, resume writers, articles, and links to resources (executive recruiters, newspapers, magazines, search engines, universities) in eight countries of the Americas. An excellent resource for bilingual job seekers.

Hire Diversity.com	**Minorities**
www.hirediversity.com	

Offers special diversity channels for African Americans, Asian Americans, people with disabilities, gays and lesbians, Hispanics, mature workers, Native Americans, veterans, and women. Includes nearly 15,000 job postings and more than 100,000 resumes in its searchable database. Job seekers can search the job database by area of expertise and location. This site also includes separate sections on corporations, government, nonprofits, education, and entrepreneurship as well as headline news and a newsletter.

DiversityLink.com	**Minorities**
diversitylink.com	

Targets female, minority, and other diversity professionals. Includes a resume database, job postings, profiles of candidates, featured employers, and a list of supporting organizations.

Other useful minority and diversity sites, many of which tend to specialize on a particular minority or diversity issue, include:

- Africareers.com   www.africareers.com
- Asia-Net.com   www.asia-net.com
- Asia-Jobs.com   www.asia-jobs.com
- Best Diversity Employers   www.bestdiversityemployers.com
- Black Collegian   www.blackcollegian.com
- Blackenterprise.com   www.blackenterprise.com
- Black Voices   http://new.blackvoices.com/ classified/jobs
- CareerMoves (Jewish)   www.jvsjobs.org

- ChristiaNet (Religious)   www.christianet.com/christianjobs
- ChristianJobs (Religious)   www.christianjobs.com
- Corporate Diversity Search   www.corpdiversitysearch.com
- CVLatino (Hispanic)   http://cvlatino.com
- DiversiLink (Hispanic)   www.diversilink.com
- Diversity Job Network   www.diversityjobnetwork.com
- Diversity Recruiting   www.diversityrecruiting.com
- Diversity Search.com   www.diversitysearch.com
- DiversityWorking   www.diversityworking.com
- EOP Online   www.eop.com
- Gaywork.com (Gays)   www.gaywork.com
- Global Mission (Religious)   www.globalmission.org
- HireDiversity   www.hirediversity.com
- Hispanic Online Cyber Career Center   www.hispaniconline.com
- IMdiversity.com   www.imdiversity.com
- InternationalMVP   www.career.mvp.com/foreign.htm
- Jewishcampstaff.com (Jewish)   www.jewishcampstaff.com
- JobCentro (Hispanic)   www.jobcentro.com
- JobLatino (Hispanic)   www.joblatino.com
- LatinoWeb.com (Hispanic)   www.latinoweb.com
- Ministry Connect (Religious)   www.ministryconnect.org
- MinistryJobs (Religious)   www.ministryjobs.com
- MinistrySearch.com   www.ministrysearch.com
- MinorityCareer.Com   www.minoritycareer.com
- Minority Executive Search   www.minorityexecsearch.com
- MinorityNurse.com   www.minoritynurse.com
- Multicultural Advantage   www.multiculturaladvantage.com
- NativeAmericanJobs.com   www.nativeamericanjobs.com
- Saludos.com (Hispanic)   www.saludos.com
- TodoLatino (Hispanic)   www.todolatino.com
- NativeJobs (Native-Americans)   www.nativejobs.com
- VisaJobs (Immigrants)   www.visajobs.com
- Youth Specialties (Religious)   www.youthspecialties.com
- WorkplaceDiversity.com   www.workplacediversity.com

People With Disabilities

Over 50 million people in the United States have some form of disability that may affect their work as well as their occupational choices. According to studies, everyone becomes disabled for several years during their lives, with 13 years often given as the average period for disabilities.

People with disabilities can turn to several websites for assistance. However, very few sites include resume databases and job listings for them. Unfortunately, most such websites primarily dispense information about disabilities and focus on training. But more and more websites are focusing on linking disabled job seekers with employers who actively seek to recruit such candidates.

Job Accommodation Network **www.jan.wvu.edu**	**Disabilities**

This is a gateway site for accessing numerous resources relevant to disabled people. Includes linkages to websites that specialize in particular types of disabilities, such as addictions, cardiovascular and pulmonary, musculoskeletal, psychiatric, and sensory.

Job Access **www.jobaccess.org**	**Disabilities**

This site is designed to assist job seekers in finding employment with businesses, government agencies, and nonprofit organizations. It includes a resume database, job postings, and online career fairs through its relationship with www.careerbuilder.com. Most of the job services are generic to all job seekers, regardless of disabilities.

Disabled Person **www.disabledperson.com**	**Disabilities**

This site also comes under the name of Recruitability, an online community for people with disabilities. Includes job postings, a resume database for employers and placement agencies, and job search tips. Other sections of this site include featured articles, issues and opinions, disability resources, and community events.

Other websites that also focus on the employment needs of disabled people include:

- Able to Work   www.abletowork.org
- American Association of People With Disabilities   www.aapd-dc.org
- Community Options, Inc.   www.comop.org
- Department of Labor   www.dol.gov/dol/odep/ joblinks/joblinks.htm
- Federal Jobs   www.federaljobs.net/disabled.htm
- Hire Deaf   www.hiredeaf.com
- Jobability   www.jobability.com
- National Organization on Disability   www.nod.org
- New Mobility   www.newmobility.com
- RecruitAbility   www.recruit-ability.com
- The Work Site (SSA)   www.socialsecuity.gov/work/ index.html
- Training Resource Network   www.trninc.com
- WorkSupport   www.worksupport.com
- Yourable.com   www.yourable.com

Government and Law Enforcement

If you're interested in working with government – over 20 million U.S. citizens do – you will find numerous websites focused on federal, state, and local government. While most U.S. federal, state, and local government agencies maintain their own websites, similar to the company websites of businesses, other websites bring together all of government. Several websites also focus on specialty areas, such as law enforcement, within government at all levels.

USA Jobs   **Government**
www.usajobs.opm.gov

This is the federal government's (Office of Personnel Management) gateway site to federal employment. Functions as a job board for vacancies with various federal agencies. Includes information on the application process, Senior Executive Service, student employment, veterans preference, and online applications.

Federal Jobs Central	Government
www.fedjobs.com	

Publishers of the popular *Federal Career Opportunities*, which lists vacancies with most federal agencies, this site includes one of the most comprehensive databases of current federal job openings. Includes featured agencies, pay scales, application tools, tips, and links to other resources. Operated by the highly respected Federal Research Service.

Federal Jobs Digest	Government
www.jobsfed.com	

Operated by the publishers of the long-running *Federal Jobs Digest*, this site includes a huge database of agency vacancies along with a job matching service, federal benefits, hiring news, federal resume advice, and a bookstore (includes only two of their own titles).

Lawenforcementjobs.com	Law Enforcement
www.lawenforcementjobs.com	

Primarily functions as a job board for the field of law enforcement. Includes job postings and linkages to several important resources (tests, training, degrees, and police pay). Includes a bookstore of relevant titles.

Numerous other websites also focus on government and law enforcement jobs:

- Careers in Government — www.careersingovernment.com
- Classified Employment Web Site — www.yourinfosource.com/ CLEWS
- Cop Career.com — www.copcareer.com
- Cops Online — www.copsonline.com/careers.cfm

- Corrections.com   http://database.corrections.com/
                                career
- Federal Jobs Net   www.federaljobs.net
- FederalJobSearch   www.federaljobsearch.com
- Federal Times   http://federaltimes.com
- FedGate   www.fedgate.org
- FedWorld.gov   www.fedworld.gov
- FirstGov   www.firstgov.gov
- GovernmentJobs.com   www.governmentjobs.com
- Govjobs.com   www.govjobs.com
                                www.govtjob.net
- JobCop   www.jobcop.com
- Jobs4Police   www.jobs4police.com
- Jobs4PublicSector (Europe)   www.jobs4publicsector.com
- Officer.com   www.officer.com
- PoliceCareer.com   www.policecareer.com
- Police Employment   www.policeemployment.com
- PSE-NET.com   www.PSE-NET.com
- StateJobs.com   www.statejobs.com
- United Nations   www.unsystem.org
- US Government Jobs.com   www.usgovernmentjobs.com
- US Intelligence Community   www.intelligence.gov
- White House   www.whitehouse.gov

If you're interested in working for the federal government, you may want to explore employment opportunities with these major federal agencies:

- African Development
  Foundation   www.adf.gov
- Agency for International
  Development (USAID)   www.usaid.gov
- Central Intelligence Agency   www.cia.gov
- Consumer Product Safety
  Commission   www.cpsc.gov
- Department of Agriculture   www.usda.gov
- Department of Commerce   www.commerce.gov
- Department of Defense   www.dtic.mil

- Department of Energy   www.doe.gov
- Department of Health
  and Human Services   www.os.dhhs.gov
- Department of Homeland
  Security   www.dhs.gov
- Department of Justice   www.usdoj.gov
- Department of State   www.state.gov
- Department of
  Transportation   www.dot.gov
- Environmental Protection
  Agency   www.epa.gov
- Export-Import Bank   www.exim.gov
- Federal Communications
  Commission   www.fcc.gov
- Federal Emergency
  Management Agency   www.fema.gov
- General Services
  Administration   www.gsa.gov
- Inter-American Foundation   www.iaf.gov
- Internal Revenue Service   www.irs.ustreas.gov
- Peace Corps   www.peacecorps.com
- Smithsonian Institution   www.si.edu
- U.S. Postal Service   www.usps.gov

Nonprofit Sector

The U.S. nonprofit sector employs over 10 million people in the United States and abroad. It offers numerous opportunities for people interested in pursuing a cause and helping people. Initially slow to use the Internet, the nonprofit sector has increasingly become active in recruiting online. The following sites function as gateways to the employment world of the nonprofit sector.

GuideStar   **Nonprofits**
www.guidestar.org

This is the ultimate gateway site for researching the nonprofit sector. Includes a database of more than 850,000 U.S. nonprofit organizations. Use the search engine to find a nonprofit that fits your particular interests. Previously featured on page 121.

Action Without Borders	**Nonprofits**
www.idealist.org	

If you are interested in international nonprofit organizations, it doesn't get any better than this gateway site to jobs with international nonprofits. Includes links to thousands of job resources in 165 countries. Offers job postings, a "push" email service, and newsletter. Resources cover organizations, jobs, volunteering, services, campaigns, events, internships, career affairs, career information, and tools for organizations.

Several of the following websites function as gateways to thousands of nonprofit organizations:

- **Charity Village**   www.charityvillage.com
- **Council on Foundations**   www.cof.org
- **Foundation Center**   www.fdncenter.org
- **Independent Sector**   www.independentsector.org
- **Internet Nonprofit Center** www.nonprofits.org
- **VolunteerMatch**   www.volunteermatch.org

The following websites function as job boards for nonprofits. They include hundreds of job vacancy announcements:

- **Community Career Center** www.nonprofitjobs.org
- **Jobs in Nonprofit**   www.jobsinnonprofit.com
- **Nonprofit Jobs**   www.nonprofit-jobs.org

After exploring the gateway nonprofit sites and major job boards, consider including the following websites in your research:

- **AIESEC**   www.aiesec.org
- **Global Health Council**   www.globalhealth.org
- **IAESTE**   www.iaeste.org
- **InterAction**   www.interaction.org

- Intercristo   www.jobleads.org
- International Service
  Agencies   www.charity.org
- JustAct (Youth Action
  for Global Justice)   www.justact.org
- PACT   www.pactworld.com
- Volunteers for Peace   www.vfp.org
- World Learning   www.worldlearning.org

Some of the major nonprofit organizations that also maintain informative websites include:

- Academy for Educational
  Development   www.aed.org
- ACCION International   www.accion.org
- Adventist Development and
  Relief Agency International   www.adra.org
- Africare, Inc.   www.africare.org
- Agricultural Co-op
  Development International   www.acdivoca.org
- Air Serv International   www.airserv.org
- American Friends
  Service Committee   www.afsc.org
- American Jewish Joint
  Distribution Committee   www.ajc.org
- American Red Cross
  International Services   www.redcross.org/services/intl
- AmeriCares Foundation   www.americares.org
- Amnesty International (USA)   www.amnestyusa.org
- Asia Foundation   www.asiafoundation.org
- Battelle Memorial Institute   www.battelle.org
- Bread for the World   www.bread.org
- Brother's Brother
  Foundation   www.brothersbrother.org
- CARE   www.care.org
- Catholic Relief Services   www.catholicrelief.org
- Centre for Development
  and Population Activities   www.cedpa.org

- Childreach   www.childreach.org
- Christian Children's Fund   www.christianchildrensfund.org
- Church World Service   www.churchworldservice.org
- Compassion International   www.compassion.com
- Direct Relief International   www.directrelief.org
- Doctors Without Borders   www.doctorswithoutborders.org
- Educational Development Center   http://main.edc.org
- Family Health International   www.fhi.org
- Food for the Hungry, Inc.   www.fh.org
- Global Health Council   www.globalhealth.org
- Greenpeace   www.greenpeaceusa.org
- Habitat for Humanity International   www.habitat.org
- Heifer Project International   www.heifer.org
- Helen Keller International   www.hki.org
- The Hunger Project   www.thp.org
- Institute of International Education   www.iie.org
- InterExchange   www.interexchange.org
- International Aid, Inc.   www.internationalaid.org
- International Catholic Migration Commission   www.icmc.net
- International Development Enterprises   www.ideorg.org
- International Executive Service Corps   www.iesc.org
- International Eye Foundation   www.iefusa.org
- International Institute of Rural Reconstruction   www.panasia.org.sg/iirr
- International Rescue Committee   www.theirc.org
- LASPAU – Academic and Professional Programs for the Americas   www.laspau.harvard.edu
- Laubach Literacy International   www.proliteracy.org

- Lutheran Immigration
  and Refugee Service   www.lirs.org
- Lutheran World Relief   www.lwr.org
- MAP International   www.map.org
- Mennonite Central
  Committee   www.mcc.org
- Mercy Corps International   www.mercycorps.org
- MidAmerica International
  Agricultural Consortium   www.miac.org
- National Cooperative
  Business Association   www.cooperative.org
- National Wildlife
  Federation   www.nwf.org
- The Nature Conservancy   http://nature.org
- OIC (Opportunities
  Industrial Centers)
  International   www.oicinternational.org
- Operation USA   www.opusa.org
- Opportunity International   www.opportunity.org
- Oxfam America   www.oxfamamerica.org
- PACT (Private Agencies
  Collaborating Together)   www.pactworld.org
- Partners of the Americas   www.partners.net
- Pathfinder International   www.pathfind.org
- People to People Health
  Foundation (Project HOPE)   www.projecthope.org
- PLAN International   www.plan-international.org
- Planned Parenthood
  Federation   www.plannedparenthood.org
- Population Action
  International   www.populationaction.org
- Population Council   www.popcouncil.org
- Population Reference
  Bureau   www.prb.org
- Population Services
  International   www.psi.org
- Program for Appropriate
  Technology in Health   www.path.org

- Project Concern
  International   www.projectconcern.org
- Research Triangle Institute   www.rti.org
- Salvation Army World
  Service Office   www2.salvationarmy.org
- Save the Children
  Foundation, Inc.   www.savethechildren.org
- The Sierra Club   www.sierraclub.org
- TechnoServe   www.technoserve.org
- U.S. Catholic Conference
  Office of Migration
  and Refugee Services   www.nccbuscc.org/mrs
- U.S. Committee for UNICEF   www.unicefusa.org
- Unitarian Universalist
  Service Committee   www.uusc.org
- Volunteers in Overseas
  Cooperative Assistance   www.acdivoca.org
- Volunteers in Technical
  Assistance   www.vita.org
- Winrock International
  Institute for Agricultural
  Development   www.winrock.org
- World Concern   www.worldconcern.org
- World Council of
  Credit Unions   www.woccu.org
- World Education   www.worlded.org
- World Relief Corporation   www.worldrelief.org
- World Resources Institute   www.wri.org
- World Vision Relief and
  Development, Inc.   www.worldvision.org
- World Wildlife Fund   www.wwf.org
- Worldteach   www.worldteach.org
- Worldwatch Institute   www.worldwatch.org
- Y.M.C.A.   www.ymca.com
- Y.W.C.A.   www.ywca.org
- Zero Population Growth   www.zpg.org

The following nonprofit research, educational, and trade organizations and associations variously function as think tanks, lobbying groups, and training organizations. Most of these nonprofits do a great deal of international work:

- American Enterprise
  Institute (AEI)   www.aei.org
- Brookings Institution   www.brook.edu
- CATO Institute   www.cato.org
- Center for Strategic and
  International Studies   www.csis.org
- Chamber of Commerce   www.uschamber.org
- Council for International
  Exchange of Scholars   www.cies.org
- Council of the Americas   www.counciloftheamericas.org
- Council on Foreign Relations   www.cfr.org
- Council on International
  Educational Exchange   www.ciee.org
- Earthwatch Institute   www.earthwatch.org
- Foreign Policy Association   www.fpa.org
- Freedom House   www.freedomhouse.org
- Heritage Foundation   www.heritage.org
- Hoover Institute on War,
  Revolution, and Peace   www.hoover.org
- Human Rights Watch   www.hrw.org
- The International Center   www.internationalcenter.com
- International Food Policy
  Research Institute   www.cgiar.org
- International Schools
  Services   www.iss.edu
- Meridian International
  Center   www.meridian.org
- NAFSA/Association of
  International Educators   www.nafsa.org
- Near East Foundation   www.neareast.org
- Network for Change   www.envirolink.org
- Overseas Development
  Council   www.odc.org

- RAND Corporation   www.rand.org
- U.S.-China Business Council   www.uschina.org
- United States Olympic
  Committee   www.usoc.org
- The Urban Institute   www.urban.org
- World Learning   www.worldlearning.org
- World Neighbors   www.wn.org
- Youth for Understanding
  International Exchange   www.yfu.org

For more information on opportunities with nonprofit organizations, see our companion volume, *Jobs and Careers With Nonprofit Organizations* (Impact Publications, 1999).

International Job Seekers

Individuals interested in international jobs tend to have a passion for working in the international arena. The passion is usually related to a particular region, country, or culture. Given the seeming difficulty in locating and communicating with international employers, the Internet has begun to play an increasingly important role in an international job search. Job seekers and employers can now quickly connect with each other and communicate by email and conduct online interviews. In addition to the many nonprofit international sites identified in the previous section, several other websites primarily focus on international jobs.

EscapeArtist.com   **International**
www.escapeartist.com

This is the ultimate gateway site to the international arena. It's jam-packed with just about everything you ever wanted to know about moving, living, working, investing, and retiring abroad. It's a no-nonsense site that delivers lots of great content: *"We don't have a lot of nonsense about culture shock and 'how to keep in contact with home' chat-baloney. If you want to go, go; if you want to whimper, stay home. Home is where the heart's on fire."* The site includes extensive sections on international jobs. You can easily spend hours getting lost and found on this site. If there only is one international website you use, make sure it's this one.

| Overseas Jobs | International |
| **www.overseasjobs.com** | |

This well organized site includes numerous searchable international job listings as well as a resume database (through the AboutJobs.com database). Offers company profiles, job search tips, mailing list, and links to related sites in its network.

| Monster Work Abroad | International |
| **http://workabroad.monster.com** | |

Another Monster.com specialty website, which includes a large database of international jobs, a huge resume database, expert advice, boards, and articles. Includes job search tips and resources for improving an international job search. One of the best international job sites on the web. It appeals to a wide range of international job seekers, from entry level to senior level and consultants.

| JobsAbroad.com | International |
| **www.jobsabroad.com** | |

This site especially appeals to college students and recent graduates who want to work, study, and/or travel abroad. Includes information on internships, language schools, volunteering abroad, teaching abroad, and travel. Its jobs section includes job postings and linkages to country-specific sites.

| Transitions Abroad | International |
| **www.transitionsabroad.com** | |

A very popular site for students and others interested in work, study, and alternative travel. Packed with information and resources for anyone interested in internships abroad, teaching English, volunteering abroad, and responsible travel. Publishes the popular *Transitions Abroad* magazine.

iAgora.com   International
www.iagora.com

This site functions as an international community for exchanging information and advice on working, living, and studying abroad. Includes lots of useful job search tips, discussion groups, resources, and links. A great place to do global networking.

Going Global   International
www.goinglobal.com

Launched in December 2001, this relatively new site is operated by Mary Anne Thompson, author of the popular *The Global Resume and CV Guide* and the newly released *Going Global Career Guide* (available online through Impact's bookstore, www.impactpublications.com). The site extends the baseline work presented in her books on individual country employment profiles. Users can preview more than 25 country guides online – each of which run 50 to 75 pages when printed out – as well as purchase them in the form of e-books for $14.95 each. Individual country profiles examine key employment issues as well as cover work permits, visa regulations, key employers, employment websites, local recruitment firms, and more. The site also includes tips on writing resumes and CVs, links to career professionals in each country (local advisor teams of career professionals), a newsletter, hot topics, and a global forum (message board). Primarily focusing on offering international job information, advice, consultation, and contacts on specific countries, the site does not include a job board nor a resume database. You'll need to click on partner sites in order to access such functions. A good site for organizing a job search targeted on specific countries.

Other useful international employment-related sites include the following:

- AboutJobs.com   www.aboutjobs.com
- ActiJob.com   www.actijob.com
- Alliances Abroad   www.alliancesabroad.com

- BackdoorJobs   www.backdoorjobs.com
- Dave's ESL Café   www.eslcafe.com
- Expat Exchange   www.expatexchange.com
- Expatica   www.expatica.com/jobs
- Global Career Center   www.globalcareercenter.com
- GoAbroad   www.goabroad.com
- Heidrick & Struggles   www.heidrick.com
- International Career
  Employment Center   www.internationaljobs.org
- International Staffing
  Consultants   www.iscworld.com
- International Resources   www.umich.edu/~icenter/
  (key resource site)   overseas/work/index.html
- Job Monkey.com   www.jobmonkey.com
- JobsBazaar.com   www.jobsbazaar.com
- Jobpilot.com   www.jobpilot.net
- Jobshark.com   www.jobshark.com
- Jobs.Net   www.jobs.net
- JobsDB.com   www.jobsdb.com
- Jobware International   www.jobware.com
- Korn/Ferry International   www.ekornferry.com
- Nicholson International   www.nicholsonintl.com
- Management Recruiters
  International   www.brilliantpeople.com
- PlanetRecruit   www.planetrecruit.com
- PricewaterhouseCoopers   www.pwcglobal.com
- Riley Guide   www.rileyguide.com/internat.html
- Spencer Stuart   www.spencerstuart.com
- Teaching Jobs Overseas   www.joyjobs.com
- Top Jobs   www.topjobs.net
- Workopolis.com (Canada)   www.workopolis.com
- WorldWorkz   www.worldworkz.com

The largest number of websites for international job seekers are regional or country-specific, such as www.africajobs.net, www.asia-net.com, www.asiadragons.com, www.careerone.com.au (Australia), www.jobscanada.com, www.eurojobs.com, www.southamericajobs.net, www.arabiajobs.net, and Monster.com's 16 country-specific websites. We outline over

1,400 international-related sites, including several international head-hunter sites, in a separate companion volume, *The Directory of Websites for International Jobs* (Impact Publications, 2002).

Part-Time, Temporary, and Contract

During the past decade, the number of part-time, temporary, and contract employees has increased substantially. As a result, more and more staffing agencies have extended their services over the Internet. In addition to the temporary staffing agencies, such as Net-Temps, Robert Half International, Manpower, and Kelly Services, outlined in Chapter 13 (pages 177-179), the following websites are especially popular with individuals and employers interested in part-time, temporary, or contract work. Many of these sites specialize in IT workers who often prefer project-based contract arrangements to full-time jobs.

eWork www.ework.com	Free Agents

Claiming more than 300,000 registered users in its talent market database, this site attempts to match the projects of hiring managers with independent professionals and small services firms that have the necessary skills. The site also includes newsletters, featured articles, and online courses. eWork also provides employers with payroll, benefits, and related personnel services.

Numerous other websites offer services for a wide range of free agents who want to work part-time or as contract workers:

- **Aquent Talent Finder**   www.aquent.com
- **Consultants-On-Demand**   www.consultants-on-demand.com
- **ContractJobHunter**   www.cjhunter.com
- **Contractorforum.com**   www.contractorforum.com
- **Dice.com**   www.dice.com
- **Do a Project**   www.doaproject.com
- **eLance**   www.elance.com
- **eMoonlighter.com**   www.emoonlighter.com
  (becomes Guru on 1/1/04)   www.guru.com

- FreeAgent.com   www.freeagent.com
- Handyman.com   www.handyman.com
- HireAbility   www.hireability.com
- Icplanet   www.icplanet.com
- Itmoonlighter.com   www.itmoonlighter.com
- MBA Free Agents.com   www.mbaglobalnet.com/free
                                agents.html
- Subcontract.com   www.subcontract.com
- Talentmarket.monster.com   www.talentmarket.monster.com
- Parttimejobstore.com   www.parttimejobstore.com
- Software Contractor's Guild   www.scguild.com
- Swiftwork   www.swiftwork.com
- TalentGateway   www.talentgateway.com
- UBidContract.com   www.ubidontract.com
- Unicru   www.unicru.com

Freelancers and Telecommuters

Freelancers and telecommuters are a special type of free agents. Many of them are writers and designers who work on special stories and projects. Many also are work-at-home moms who create their own small businesses or acquire telecommuting jobs that range from telemarketing and customer service jobs operated from call centers to computer programming and online marketing conducted from homes. The following sites reveal numerous opportunities for these types of free agents who constitute a large segment of the working population. Indeed, some studies estimate that more than 20 million people in the United States may work in these nontraditional work settings.

| MoneyFromHome.com   Home-Based Work |
| www.moneyfromhome.com |

Posts jobs of interest to home-based workers. Screens legitimate versus scam operations that often plague this employment arena. Includes a special section for moms, profiles of successful home workers, andfrequently asked questions. Individuals pay an annual membership fee of $35 to access this site.

| **Sologig.com** | **Freelancers** |
| **www.sologig.com** | |

Designed for experienced freelancers, consultants, and independent professionals who wish to connect with some of the country's top employers and recruiters, this site includes a resume database and project listings. The resource center links to a popular assessment website (www.assessment.com) and a consortium of online universities, University Alliance Online.

The following websites provide a wealth of information on freelancing, telecommuting, and home-based jobs:

- All Freelance   www.allfreelance.com
- FreelanceJobSearch.com   www.freelancejobsearch.com
- FreelanceOnline.com   www.freelanceonline.com
- Freelance Work Exchange   www.freelanceworkexchange.com
- FreelanceWriting.com   www.freelancewriting.com
- Freetimejobs.com   www.freetimejobs.com
- Homeworking.com   www.homeworking.com
- Institute of Management Consultants   www.imcusa.org
- MediaStreet.com   www.mediastreet.com
- OutSource 2000   www.outsource2000.com
- PortaJobs   www.portajobs.com
- ProsForHire.com   www.prosforhire.com
- Smarterwork.com   www.smarterwork.com
- Telecommuting Jobs   www.tjobs.com
- Telework Connection   www.telework-connection.com
- Womans-Work.com   www.womans-work.com
- Work at Home Moms   www.wahm.com
- WorkOnLine   http://telecommute.hypermart.net

Spooks, Spies, and Intel Specialists

Even spies need jobs! Indeed, with the ending of the Cold War more than a decade ago, many individuals in the intelligence community found themselves in a very different job market. A very special group known for

their unique technical skills, high levels of job satisfaction, and comara-
derie, many of these individuals regularly leave the closed worlds,
including the "black" services, of federal security agencies and the military
and transition to the private sector. Many of the resources identified in
the "Military Transition" section (pages 218-222) are relevant to this
special group of job seekers who increasingly gravitate to intelligence and
security jobs in the private sector. For information on the government-
based intelligence community, be sure to visit this community gateway
website:

www.intelligence.gov

The following websites, many of which provide excellent networking
opportunities for this closely knit community, are especially relevant to
job seekers seeking jobs and careers in intelligence:

Intelligence Careers   **Intelligence**
www.intelligencecareers.com

Offers searchable job listings and a resume database for information and intelligence specialists. Includes news and linkages to
other employment websites for career advice, internships, law
enforcement jobs, intelligence topics, and newsletters. A calendar
of upcoming career events (organized for cleared candidates and
general public) is well worth checking out since these events are
often critical to landing intel jobs.

Other websites of interest to anyone seeking a job in intelligence
services includes:

- **Armed Forces
  Communications Electronics
  Association**   www.afcea.org
- **Association of Former
  Intelligence Officers**   www.afio.com
- **Association of Old Crows**   www.aochq.org
- **Defense Advanced Research
  Project Agency**   www.arpa.gov
- **Central Intelligence Agency**   www.cia.gov

- Federal Bureau of
  Investigation (FBI)   www.fbi.gov
- Infowar.com   www.infowar.com
- International Association of
  Counterterrorism and
  Security Personnel   www.iacsp.com
- International Association of
  Law Enforcement
  Intelligence Analysts   www.ialeia.org
- IT Toolbox Security   www.security.ittoolbox.com
- National Security Agency   www.nsa.gov
- National Security Institute   www.nsi.org
- PCIC.net   www.pcic.net
- Society of Competitive
  Intelligence Professionals   www.scip.org
- Society of Former Special
  Agents of the FBI   www.socxfbi.org
- Special Forces Association   www.sfahq.org

Ex-Offenders in Transition

Incarceration is both a big problem and a big business in the U.S. Over
2 million people are currently residing in prisons or jails. Each year nearly
600,000 individuals are released after having served time for various
criminal acts. The majority (over 60 percent) are drug-related cases. In
New York City alone nearly 125,000 individuals are released each year.
At any one time nearly 4 million adults are on probation and 700,000 on
parole. Not surprisingly, few employers are eager to assist this group of
job seekers. Indeed, as soon as an ex-offender tells the truth on an
application about his or her criminal record, many employers automatically disqualify them from further consideration. The number one
problem for many ex-offenders upon being released is to find a steady and
rewarding job. Often viewed as the dregs of society – the last hired and
the first fired – nearly 70 percent of these individuals lose their jobs
within the first 60 days after landing a job. Lacking employment and
repeating past patterns of criminal behavior, many of these ex-offenders
commit crimes and eventually return to prison or jail. Unfortunately,
there are few community-based support services to help this group of job

seekers find employment. Local churches, shelters, and nonprofit organizations provide some assistance. Occasionally the Federal Bureau of Prisons and nonprofit organizations host special job fairs for ex-offenders. While few websites are designed to help them with employment, some sites try to assist this very special and difficult to place group of job seekers. If you are an ex-offender, or if you know someone with such a background, please visit these websites. They could possibly change lives:

- American Correctional
  Association   www.aca.org
- American Jail Association   www.corrections.com/aja
- American Probation and
  Parole Association   www.appa-net.org
- Better People   www.betterpeople.org
- Family and Corrections
  Network   www.fcnetwork.org
- Family ReEntry, Inc.   www.familyreentry.org
- Goodwill Industries   www.goodwill.org
- Hope for Ex-Criminals   www.stormloader.com/record
                                 hope.html
- Impact Publications
  (See "Ex-Offenders")   www.impactpublications.com
- Labor Finders   www.laborfinders.com
- National Institute of
  Corrections   www.nicic.org
- Northern California   www.norcalserviceleague.org/
  Service League   jobplace.htm
- Open Inc.   www.openinc.org
- Osborne Association/   www.osborneny.org/south_forty.
  South Forty   htm
- Prison Fellowship Ministries   www.pfm.org
- Prison Links   www.prisonlinks.com
- Project RIO   www.workforcelink.com.html/
                                 rio/default_rio.html
- UNICOR Placement   www.unicor.gov/placement/
                                 ippeopp.htm
- Vera Institute of Justice   www.vera.org
- Welcome Home Ministries   www.welcomehomeministries.
                                 com

Index

249

The Authors

FOR MORE THAN TWO DECADES Ron and Caryl Krannich have pursued a passion – assisting hundreds of thousands of individuals, from students, the unemployed, and ex-offenders to military personnel, international job seekers, and CEOs, in making critical job and career transitions. Focusing on key job search skills, career changes, and employment fields, their impressive body of work has helped shape career thinking and behavior both in the United States and abroad. Their sound advice has changed numerous lives, including their own!

Ron and Caryl are two of America's leading career and travel writers who have authored more than 60 books. A former Peace Corps Volunteer and Fulbright Scholar, Ron received his Ph.D. in Political Science from Northern Illinois University. Caryl received her Ph.D. in Speech Communication from Penn State University. Together they operate Development Concepts Incorporated, a training, consulting, and publishing firm in Virginia.

The Krannichs are both former university professors, high school teachers, management trainers, and consultants. As trainers and consultants, they have completed numerous projects on management, career development, local government, population planning, and rural development in the United States and abroad. Their career books focus on key job search skills, military and civilian career transitions, government and international careers, travel jobs, and nonprofit organizations and include such classics as *High Impact Resumes and Letters, Interview for Success*, and *Change Your Job, Change Your Life*.

Their books represent one of today's most comprehensive collections of career writing. With over 2 million copies in print, their publications are widely available in bookstores, libraries, and career centers. No strangers to the world of Internet employment, they have written *America's Top Internet Job Sites* and *The Directory of Websites for International Jobs* and published several Internet recruitment and job search books. Ron served as the first Work Abroad Advisor to Monster. com. They also have developed several career-related websites: www. impactpublications.com, www.winningthejob.com, www.contentforcareers .com, and www.veteransworld.com. Many of their career tips appear on such major websites as www.campuscareercenter.com, www.monster.com, www.careerbuilder.com, and www.employmentguide.com.

Ron and Caryl live a double life with travel being their best kept *"do what you love"* career secret. Authors of 19 travel-shopping guidebooks on various destinations around the world, they continue to pursue their international and travel interests through their innovative *Treasures and Pleasures of . . . Best of the Best* travel-shopping series and several related websites: www.ishoparoundtheworld.com, www.contentfortravel.com, www.hoteltravelshop.com, and www.mycruiseshop.com. When not found at their home and business in Virginia, they are probably somewhere in Europe, Asia, Africa, the Middle East, the South Pacific, or the Caribbean and South America following their other passion – researching and writing about quality arts and antiques as well as heeding the advice of their other Internet-related volume designed for road warriors and other travel types: *Travel Planning on the Internet: The Click and Easy™ Guide*. *"We follow the same career and life-changing advice we give to others – pursue a passion that enables you to do what you really love to do,"* say the Krannichs. Their passion is best represented on www.ishoparoundtheworld.com.

As both career and travel experts, the Krannichs' work is frequently featured in major newspapers, magazines, and newsletters as well as on radio, television, and the Internet. Available for interviews, consultation, and presentations, they can be contacted as follows:

Ron and Caryl Krannich
krannich@impactpublications.com

Career Resources

THE FOLLOWING CAREER RESOURCES are available directly from Impact Publications. Full descriptions of each title as well as downloadable catalogs, videos, and software can be found on our website: www.impactpublications.com. Complete the following form or list the titles, include shipping (see formula at the end), enclose payment, and send your order to:

IMPACT PUBLICATIONS
9104 Manassas Drive, Suite N
Manassas Park, VA 20111-5211 USA
1-800-361-1055 (orders only)
Tel. 703-361-7300 or Fax 703-335-9486
Email address: info@impactpublications.com
Quick & easy online ordering: www.impactpublications.com

Orders from individuals must be prepaid by check, money order, or major credit card. We accept telephone, fax, and email orders.

Qty.	TITLES	Price	TOTAL

Featured Title

	America's Top Internet Jobs Sites	$19.95	

New/Recently Published/Classics

	25 Jobs That Have It All	12.95	
	50 Cutting Edge Jobs	15.95	
	95 Mistakes Job Seekers Make and How to Avoid Them	13.95	
	101 Dynamite Questions to Ask At Your Job Interview	13.99	
	101 Secrets of Highly Effective Speakers	15.95	
	150 Great Tech Prep Careers	29.95	

_____ 201 Dynamite Job Search Letters (4ᵗʰ Edition)   19.95   _____
_____ America's Top Jobs for People Without a Four-
       Year Degree   15.95   _____
_____ Backdoor Guide to Short-Term Job Opportunities   21.95   _____
_____ Best Cover Letters for $100,000+ Jobs   24.95   _____
_____ Best KeyWords for Resumes, Covers Letters, and
       Interviews   17.95   _____
_____ Best Resumes and CVs for International Jobs   24.95   _____
_____ Best Resumes for $100,000+ Jobs   24.95   _____
_____ Best Resumes for People Without a Four-Year Degree   19.95   _____
_____ Blue Collar Resumes   11.99   _____
_____ Career Tests   12.95   _____
_____ CareerXroads   26.95   _____
_____ Change Your Job, Change Your Life (8ᵗʰ Edition)   17.95   _____
_____ Cover Letters for Dummies   16.99   _____
_____ Directory of Websites for International Jobs   19.95   _____
_____ Discover the Best Jobs for You   15.95   _____
_____ Discover What You're Best At   14.00   _____
_____ Do What You Are   18.95   _____
_____ Dressing Smart for Men   16.95   _____
_____ Dressing Smart for Women   16.95   _____
_____ Dynamite Salary Negotiations (4ᵗʰ Edition)   15.95   _____
_____ Expert Resumes for People Returning to Work   16.95   _____
_____ Foot in the Door: Networking   14.95   _____
_____ Fork in the Road: A Career Planning Guide
       for Young Adults   14.95   _____
_____ Global Career Guide   195.00 _____
_____ Global Citizen   16.95   _____
_____ Guide to Internet Job Searching   14.95   _____
_____ Haldane's Best Answers to Tough Interview
       Questions   15.95   _____
_____ Haldane's Best Cover Letters for Professionals   15.95   _____
_____ Haldane's Best Employment Websites for
       Professionals   15.95   _____
_____ Haldane's Best Resumes for Professionals   15.95   _____
_____ Haldane's Best Salary Tips for Professionals   15.95   _____
_____ High Impact Resumes and Letters (8ᵗʰ Edition)   19.95   _____
_____ How to Work a Room   14.00   _____
_____ I Don't Know What I Want, But I Know It's
       Not This   14.00   _____
_____ International Job Finder   19.95   _____
_____ Interview for Success (8ᵗʰ Edition)   15.95   _____
_____ Jobs and Careers With Nonprofit Organizations   17.95   _____
_____ Jobs and the Military Spouse (2ⁿᵈ Edition)   17.95   _____
_____ Jobs for Travel Lovers   19.95   _____
_____ Job Interview for Dummies   16.99   _____
_____ Job Search Handbook for People With Disabilities   16.95   _____
_____ Masters of Networking   16.95   _____
_____ Military Resumes and Cover Letters   21.95   _____
_____ Nail the Job Interview!   13.95   _____
_____ No One Will Hire Me!   13.95   _____
_____ Occupational Outlook Handbook   18.95   _____

____	Quit Your Job and Grow Some Hair	15.95	____
____	Resumes for Dummies	16.99	____
____	Savvy Interviewing	10.95	____
____	The Job Hunting Guide: Transitioning From College to Career	14.95	____
____	The Savvy Networker	13.95	____
____	What Color Is Your Parachute?	17.95	____
____	What Should I Do With My Life?	24.95	____
____	What Type Am I?	14.95	____
____	Who Moved My Cheese?	19.95	____

SUBTOTAL ____

Virginia residents add 4½% sales tax ____

POSTAGE/HANDLING ($5 for first

product and 8% of SUBTOTAL) $5.00

8% of SUBTOTAL -- ____

TOTAL ENCLOSED ------------------------ ____

❑ I enclose check/money order for $ _____ made payable to
IMPACT PUBLICATIONS.

❑ Please charge $ _____ to my credit card:
❑ Visa   ❑ MasterCard   ❑ American Express   ❑ Discover

Card # _____ Expiration date: _____/_____

Signature _____

SHIP TO:

NAME _____

ADDRESS _____

_____

_____